For A Better America.

Leonard Greene

THE NATIONAL TAX REBATE

A New America with Less Government

THE
NATIONAL
TAX
REBATE

A New America with Less Government

LEONARD M. GREENE

REGNERY
PUBLISHING, INC.

1947 • Celebrating 50 Years • 1997

Washington, D.C.

To the memory of my father,
who supported his family
by starting a small business.

Library of Congress Cataloging-in-Publication Data

Greene, Leonard M.
The national tax rebate: a new America with less government/
by Leonard M. Greene.
p. cm.
Includes index.
ISBN 0–89526–351–3. —ISBN 0–89526–356–4 (pbk.)
1. Tax rebates—Law and legislation—United States. 2. Taxation—Law and
legislation—United States. I. Title.
KF3569.5.Z9G74 1998
343.7305'23—dc21

98–17074
CIP

Published in the United States by
Regnery Publishing, Inc.
An Eagle Publishing Company
One Massachusetts Avenue, NW
Washington, DC 20001

Distributed to the trade by
National Book Network
4720-A Boston Way
Lanham, MD 20706

Printed on acid-free paper.
Manufactured in the United States of America

10 9 8 7 6 5 4 3 2 1

Books are available in quantity for promotional or premium use.
Write to Director of Special Sales, Regnery Publishing, Inc.,
One Massachusetts Avenue, NW , Washington, DC 20001,
for information on discounts and terms or call (202) 216-0600.

TABLE OF CONTENTS

ACKNOWLEDGMENTS

THE NATIONAL TAX REBATE is the culmination of a lifetime of thought, discussion, and extensive scholarly research. Some of the highlights have included a keynote address by Margaret Thatcher at the Institute for SocioEconomic Studies (ISES) Annual Dinner on "Do We Have Too Much Egalitarianism?"; a lecture by Jack Kemp on urban renewal and enterprise zones; and the contribution of leading business, media, and political leaders such as Senator Daniel Patrick Moynihan, John Diebold, Robert Bartley, Caspar Weinberger, and Dan Quayle in numerous ISES publications.

This book would not have been possible without the staff at ISES, who helped shape the book and read the manuscript in many drafts. I am also indebted to the following people who have helped form my thinking over the years through their friendship and scholarship: Bill Archer, Arnold Berman, Robert Bernstein, George Brockway, Walter Cronkite, Martin Edelston, Bette K. Fishbein, Barry Goldwater, Terry Greene, Robert Half, Joseph Hankin, C. Lowell Harriss, Benjamin Hooks, Bonnie Le Var, Daniel Patrick Moynihan, Richard L.

Ottinger, Nita Parekh, Arnold Shaw, Harvey Shulman, Richard Sporn, Alan Teck, Margaret Thatcher, Ralph Tryon, Gordon Weil, and Walter Williams. I wish to thank Professor Irwin Garfinkel at Columbia University's School of Social Work for research support and encouragement, and Harry Crocker and Erica Rogers at Regnery Publishing for their editorial input.

The research is cited in the notes; where no citation appears, the comment is based on personal knowledge. The views expressed in this book are my own and are not necessarily shared by any of the people or organizations I have thanked.

There are no evils in government. Its evils exist only in its abuses. If it would confine itself to equal protection, and, as Heaven does its rains, shower its favors alike on the high and the low, the rich and the poor, it would be an unqualified blessing.

—ANDREW JACKSON

CHAPTER 1

Returning Your $720 Billion

THIS BOOK IS ABOUT MONEY—an enormous amount of it: *seven hundred and twenty thousand million dollars.* That's enough to buy all the gold in the U.S. treasury sixty-five times over each year. If you are an American citizen, it's your money and, what's more, it should be yours to spend, save, or invest every single year. Right now, however, you can't spend a dime of it.

This book shows American citizens how they can get this money, all $720 billion of it, back from the federal government before it spends the money on what it thinks you need. In these pages I introduce the best strategy for doing it. It is called the National Tax Rebate. Essentially it involves the government returning to the people the wealth that has been productively generated by them. It refunds to them, *to you*, their hard-earned dollars. Scholarly studies and simple common sense converge in establishing that this $720 billion would be best spent directly by those it is intended to help: the American people.

But you may ask, what exactly does this mean to me? Imagine the following scene: you're sitting in your living room watching TV when there's a knock on the door.

You open it, and a man says, "You have just won a quarter of a million dollars."

Your first reaction is incredulity.

"Is this a lottery?" you say. "Where is Ed McMahon?"

No, you are informed, this is no lottery.

"I didn't think so, because I didn't buy a ticket. I wouldn't waste my money. But why?" you ask.

"Because," the man replies, "you are an American citizen. This is money that you are owed by the U.S. government. You earned it."

And you are then handed a promissory note for $250,000, together with your first monthly payment of $1,000. You are told that from now on you will receive these payments as long as you live.

This is not a joke. And yet, as the lottery ads like to tell you, "Your life is about to change."

The National Tax Rebate will change the life of every American for the better because it means a monthly check with no strings attached for every man, woman, and child. Specifically, the National Tax Rebate would give each adult citizen $4,000 a year and each American child $2,000 a year. That's the equivalent of a family of four winning a lottery with a $12,000 annual payment.

Here are some things you could do with the money if the government were to pay you an additional $1,000 a month: make a down payment on your first home, save for your child's education, launch a start-up business, buy a new car, take that vacation you've been putting off, save for your retirement, or buy health insurance. But these are only suggestions. It's your money to invest or spend as you please. There's no end to what you could do or how much better your life could be. The possibilities are as limitless as the human imagination itself.

Where, you then ask, would I get the funds for this generous scheme? Actually I'm not being generous at all. I would be dispensing not my money, but your money... actually, our money. Each year the government forcibly confiscates hundreds of billions of dollars from American citizens in the form of taxes. I propose that the government give much of that money back.

The figure is $720 billion. That's the amount that the federal government spends annually on social service programs. I'm not counting national defense, Social Security, Medicare, or the money that pays for the highways. Indeed my figure represents only about one-half of the total federal budget—the part that's intended to help you, the people. I believe that you could put this money to better use than the government can.

The federal government has its own idea of what to do with this money: it spends it on programs that the Washington bureaucracy regards as good for the people. Some of these programs sound good, like giving food stamps to hungry people. Many others seem ridiculous, like paying farmers not to grow crops in order to keep market prices high.

Yet whatever the merits of these ideas, there is a consensus among reasonable people that government programs are almost always expensive and poorly administered. It's not that government workers are incapable or insincere. It's just that there is no bottom line. In addition, government programs do not fit varied individual needs. Consequently, most government programs operate with the efficiency of the Department of Motor Vehicles... definitely not a place for people in a hurry.

The National Tax Rebate is a better way to use the money currently consumed by government social welfare programs. It entails taking the cash—all $720 billion—and giving it back to the American people. My premise is that the money we pay to the government in taxes is our money and we have a right as self-governing citizens to decide what to do with it. This includes the right to get some of it back in the form of a rebate.

My next assumption is that average citizens, not federal bureaucrats, are best able to figure out their own best interests and how to spend or invest their hard-earned money.

Another basic assumption is that incentives matter. As an industrialist who has managed a successful manufacturing business for more than fifty years, I know that people respond to incentives. I've seen it over and over again. A National Tax Rebate would encourage every American to work, since any increase in income above the rebate could only improve his or her lifestyle.

If you agree with these premises and think you could use an extra $1,000 each month, read on—otherwise, just keep on letting the government spend it for you.

I'll show you why my proposal makes sense. More important, I'll show that it can and has worked. The National Tax Rebate is good for the economy, good for the middle class, good for the poor, and—unless you have a peculiar aversion to dollar bills—good for you. I'll also tell you how you can make this plan a reality, and get your hands on the cash.

CHAPTER 2

The Rise of
Big Government

"GIVING MONEY AND POWER to government is like giving whiskey and car keys to teenage boys," political satirist P. J. O'Rourke once remarked. Things get messy, and the results are often deadly.

But if government is like a drunken teenager, why did we allow it to get behind the wheel in the first place, when the results were all too predictable? To piece together the facts from the wreckage, we must go back some sixty years in time.

In the 1930s the nation was confronted with the gravest fiscal crisis in its history. The stock market crashed, the economy retreated, and the United States found itself mired in the grip of an unrelenting depression. Work dried up. Misery proliferated. Never before had the nation undergone such a trial for so long. People's faith in the future crumbled. Then in a moment of self-doubt, with all the best intentions, America's political leaders changed course. Radically.

In America, deprivation of this magnitude could not possibly be allowed to exist. This plague was un-American—America was a land of opportunity, not hardship! The new thinking decided that if the economy couldn't allow every person to prosper, government would see to helping them, but temporarily of course. Otherwise, the new course would become increasingly perilous, particularly if it led to permanent dependency.

President Franklin Roosevelt, architect of government's new role, warned that "continued dependence upon relief" could induce "a spiritual and moral disintegration fundamentally destructive to the national fiber." It could undermine the human spirit. For now, though, the urgency of the situation demanded federal action. Something had to be done. President Roosevelt took the risk, creating a massive wave of new government programs.

Some thirty years later, President Lyndon Johnson further expanded the government's new mandate. Now, government would not help only those in temporary need, it would guarantee all persons a minimum standard of living. A noble aim, yes; a realistic one, no. Any person falling below a designated income threshold would qualify for assistance. Even persons outside the productive economy would be covered. Poverty would be eradicated.

★ ★ ★

TODAY, OUR LIVES ARE profoundly different as a result. We live with an increasingly paternalistic government that spends in excess of $1.7 trillion of our money each year. That amounts to more than $6,000 a year for every American man, woman, and child. With each passing year, government makes more and more decisions for us. We are told more and more things we can't do. We are given more and more things we must do. We are made to surrender more and more of our hard-earned wages to the government. In short, we've lost our freedom and our tax dollars, too. All for what? That's the vital issue of the day.

Could we do better if we made the spending decisions ourselves? Absolutely! We certainly couldn't do any worse, no matter how hard we tried. Let's take a closer look at how the government uses our tax dollars. As everyone is already familiar with the Pentagon's unique ability to pay $2,000 for $30 hinges, let's focus elsewhere.

In fiscal year 1997 the U.S. Department of Agriculture spent $40 million on tobacco price supports and crop insurance at the very moment the government was waging an escalating war against the cigarette companies in the name of children's health. Talk about shooting yourself in the foot!

Things get worse. The U.S. Forest Service spent $129 million building logging roads to allow it to sell timber at an additional loss of $38 million. No business could ever afford to do such a thing. But then again, companies have to spend their own money. Government spends yours.

What about its ability to collect its debts? A nightmare. The Department of Interior is presently owed around $2 billion in royalties by large oil companies. Rather than taking steps to collect this money, the government has signed away its rights to it in legal settlements that are referred to internally by the department as the "California Royalty Secret Deals." Government has made these oil barons a gift with our tax dollars.

Despite all of government's exertions on our behalf, and some of its efforts have undeniably been creative, government waste and misspending are all around us. In short, all we have gotten in return for the loss of our money and erosion of our freedom is a raw deal.

Is this a problem? You bet it is!

★ ★ ★

WE ALL PAY THE high cost of government. Every one of us. We fund its thousands of programs—when was the last time government asked us whether we truly wanted to buy what they were offering us?—we defray the high cost to administer those programs, and we even pay for every dollar of government waste. We pay these costs with our tax returns. We also pay them every time we go to the doctor, buy groceries, or fill our car with gas.

With its new mission during the Depression and after, government embarked on an unequaled expansion. And as the government grew larger year after year, so did our tax burden. Even as income tax rates came down, new taxes sprouted up and older ones rose. Payroll taxes, for example, were increased seventeen times in the last forty years. No matter how you looked at it, once all our taxes were taken into consideration, our tax bill only grew.

Today, according to the Tax Foundation, the average family must work until May 9 just to pay its tax bill. In effect, we work nearly one out of every three days for the government. Once the cost of government regulation is factored in, each American winds up working more than half the year for the government. Put another way, Americans work every morning for the government. It is only after lunch that we work for our families and for ourselves. That's painful. Wouldn't you like to work more for yourself and family and less for the government? I know I would.

The average two-earner family's tax bill now consumes nearly 40 percent of its budget. This is more than the total devoted to food, clothing, and transportation combined! For many families, the income tax is no longer the biggest culprit. Currently, more than one in two Americans pays more in payroll taxes than in income taxes.

Who works for whom today? Does the government work for us? Or do we work for the government? Sadly, it is debatable. Worse still, every day we work more for the government and less for ourselves.

The steep financial imposition big government places on our shoulders is only part of the story. Big government's shadow darkens every aspect of our lives. It diminishes our standard of living. We have less to spend on recreation, less to invest for our son's or daughter's college education, less to put toward the purchase of a new home, less to save for retirement, less to spend on health insurance, and less to start up a business. Always less. Never more.

Big government also feasts on our hopes for the future. The cost in terms of our lost tax dollars is steep. The cost of our lost opportunities is even higher... far higher. If only we had our tax dollars to spend, save, or invest as we see fit. Imagine how much better off we'd be ten, twenty, or even thirty years from now. Too bad. We'll never know that better future. Big government has deprived us of our biggest opportunities and best hopes.

Unfortunately for us, the government's feeding frenzy doesn't stop at our paychecks. It extends all the way to our most basic freedoms. We are told what kind of business we can and can't start. We are told how we can and can't lead our lives. Our state and local governments are given federal mandates without the requisite funding. Our poor are given government assistance at the terrible price of losing their ability to make their own decisions.

Indeed, European economist Wilhelm Ropke observed, more than forty years ago, that any welfare state "covers the surface of society with a network of small complicated rules, minute and uniform, through which the most original minds and the most energetic characters cannot penetrate, to rise above the crowd. The will of man is not shattered, but softened, bent, and guided.... Such a power does not destroy, but it prevents existence; it does not tyrannize, but it compresses, enervates, extinguishes, and stupefies a people, till each nation is reduced to nothing better than a flock of timid and industrious animals, of which the government is the shepherd." Few things could be more dehumanizing than a full-blown welfare state.

As government's appetite for our tax dollars grows more and more voracious, it eats away at our most cherished rights and privileges. In the United States, we have always been presumed innocent until proven guilty. Until now. When it comes to taxes, we are presumed guilty until proven innocent. Small businesses that create two-thirds of all new jobs are particularly prone to victimization, as they have the least ability to fight back. Now *that's* some reward for the beneficial role they play in our economy!

Big government's yoke is heavy, too heavy. And for the middle class, the heart of our society, its burden is heaviest of all. Any government, regardless of how well-intentioned, that saps our ability to pursue our dreams and steals our most precious freedoms is bad government.

President Ronald Reagan memorably observed that big government lives by three simple rules of thumb: "If it moves, tax it. If it keeps moving, regulate it. And if it stops moving, subsidize it." That's the government we have today.

By any definition, today's paternalistic government is bad government. The price we pay each day for our government is far too high; the value we receive is far too low.

★ ★ ★

PERHAPS WE MIGHT not be struggling with big government over our tax dollars and the ability to make free choices had the government's efforts to help us attain a minimum standard of living succeeded. But they didn't. Despite more than $5 trillion in expenditures, poverty won. The current poverty rate of 12.7 percent is about the same as it was in 1967. Where's the progress?

Far from saving its intended beneficiaries from hardship, the welfare system's "safety net" trapped them in dependency. It cut them off from opportunity. It exacerbated destructive social pathologies, such as out-of-wedlock births, that will have a corrosive societal impact for years to come.

"The welfare culture tells the man he is not a necessary part of the family; he feels dispensable, his wife knows he is dispensable, his children sense it," noted economist Milton Friedman observed. Welfare impairs the family. By doing so, it corrupts the values essential to personal well-being. Further, it prevents even the basic notion of "right" and "wrong" from being transmitted from one generation to the next. And once these values are lost, they are difficult to restore. The *Los Angeles Times*, no instrument of conservatism, correctly noted in 1969 that government "cannot provide values to persons who have none, or who have lost those they had." Well said.

At the same time, welfare created perverse incentives that undermined people's ability to free themselves from dependency. Suddenly, welfare recipients found themselves better off receiving federal assistance than working at an entry-level job. A 1995 Cato Institute study found that, after taxes, welfare paid better than many jobs. In eight states, its benefits were worth more than the starting salary of a teacher. In twenty-eight states, they exceeded the starting salary for a secretary. In all but four states, welfare recipients could do better than janitors.

Even then, some welfare recipients fought to free themselves from the meshes of their "safety nets." "What use is a life when one is enslaved in dependency," they figured. But for daring to pursue work, they were punished by effective marginal tax rates that exceeded 100 percent.

"My husband works from 4 AM to 9 PM," a caller explained to talk show host Rush Limbaugh. "The only assistance we need is Medicaid for the kids. But if my husband gets one more raise, the kids will lose it." In another outrageous example, a Wisconsin man who worked half-time at minimum wage was forced to turn down a full-time job when he found that he would lose $1,200 more in government benefits than he would receive in additional after-tax income. I even had a young employee who quit after three months when his family faced the cruel consequences—losing its subsidized housing if he continued to work. Welfare's message is all too clear. Don't work hard, or at all, or you'll pay for it! New York University's Lawrence Mead found that welfare benefits typically cause recipients to work 30 percent less. Under those circumstances, there could be no independence from the welfare black hole. Once you are sucked in, chances are you won't escape.

According to *The 1996 Green Book*, the average length of stay for families enrolled at any given moment on welfare is thirteen years; 93 percent of these families spend three or more years on welfare; 82 percent spend five or more years on welfare; and 65 percent spend eight or more years on welfare. As horrific as these statistics are, they are hardly surprising. Welfare's permanent guarantee coupled with its financial generosity created an ideal environment for cultivating dependency.

"It's like a drug addiction," says former welfare mother Diane Lewis of Hartford, Connecticut. "I'm still sort of craving to stay in my home. I'm not lazy. I'm not stupid. I got used to a certain lifestyle." Welfare's harsh reality became abundantly clear to Ms. Lewis one day when her son refused to take out the trash. "Why should I," asked the youngster, "when you just sit at home all day?" That was it. From that moment, Ms. Lewis resolved to find a job and create a new life for herself and her son. With considerable effort and not a little anguish, she succeeded.

Surely, welfare dependency should not have become commonplace. Welfare, after all, was originally tax meant to be temporary assistance. But as has too often been the case, "temporary" is not part of the government's vocabulary. There is no greater oxymoron than temporary government assistance or temporary government program. How could welfare be temporary assistance? No bureaucracy could ever advocate a system that would eventually render it unnecessary. The welfare bureaucracy needed a permanent caseload if it was to survive. Not only that, it needed a growing caseload if it, too, was to grow. And that's exactly what happened. And we're all paying a terrible price for it.

Finally, welfare failed because it destroyed people's ability to take control of their own lives, make their own decisions, and address their own distinct needs. It was assumed that the poor were incapable of making sound decisions, much less good ones. They could not be trusted with cash. They had to be protected from themselves.

Hence the introduction of in-kind services: food stamps that could be redeemed only for food, along with day care services, housing assistance, legal services, government-run job training, and health services—none of which could be redeemed for cash. It's as if your employer thought you so irresponsible that he sent part of your paycheck to your landlord, another part to your grocer, another to the bank that provided your car loan, and still another to your physician. By 1994 there were eighty-one income-tested social programs costing more than $300 billion each year.

With a "safety net" like welfare, it is little wonder that

THE NATIONAL TAX REBATE

poverty triumphed in the war on poverty. "We tried to provide more for the poor and produced more poor instead," wrote noted social scientist Charles Murray. "We tried to remove the barrier to escape poverty, and inadvertently built a trap."

From the start, the war on poverty was never winnable. Fighting poverty by penalizing work is no different than fighting illegitimacy by banning marriage. Fighting poverty by breaking the human spirit as welfare has done is tantamount to waging war while waving a white flag. Accordingly, instead of eliminating poverty, welfare perpetuated it.

★ ★ ★

EARLY ON, THERE WERE some successes in the war on poverty. The poverty rate did decline to under 10 percent by 1972, and remained below 10 percent for most of the rest of the 1970s, even as it began a gradual ascent starting after 1974. Soon it became increasingly evident that the war on poverty would be lost. Even as government social assistance spending increased year after year, poverty counterattacked. Slowly but inexorably, poverty gained ground. At the end of 1997 the poverty rate stood at 12.7 percent, roughly the same as in 1967 in the early days of the war on poverty.

At the same time that poverty was regaining the initiative, increasing numbers of people were losing faith in the government's ability to solve problems. All they could see was the government taking an increasing share of their hard-earned tax dollars. Family budgets were being squeezed tighter and tighter by the tax collector. Family finances were being sucked up by a welfare state whose appetite was growing bigger by the day. Everywhere, the financial freedom of America's families, the key to the pursuit of happiness, was in danger. And the government could show little in return for its increasingly confiscatory policies. "There must be a better way," the people reasoned.

The broken welfare system had to be fixed. And, supposedly, it has been. On August 22, 1996, historic welfare reform legislation was signed into law. Welfare as we knew it was no more. The permanent entitlement to cash aid was gone. In its place were two block grants. One was to be used by the states to help families escape welfare (not poverty). The other was to be used by the states to help them subsidize child care for families on or leaving welfare, as well as low-income families in general. For the first time since the introduction of welfare assistance, welfare recipients would be confronted by time limits. After five years, recipients could no longer receive welfare benefits (20 percent, though, could be exempted from this restriction). At the same time, the new law created work requirements under which half of all recipients would eventually be required to engage in some form of work activity.

Unfortunately, despite the fanfare that accompanied its approval, the long-term prognosis for the new welfare law is not good. Welfare reform, no matter how bold or far-reaching, cannot create new opportunities. It can only restore existing ones. The new legislation does nothing to make entry-level work more liveable. It does nothing to relieve taxpayers of the high cost of sustaining the welfare state. In reality, it will have only a modest positive impact. Much more remains to be done.

★ ★ ★

MAYBE TAX REFORM is the way to go. What better symbol of an out-of-control government is there than a Byzantine tax code that punishes virtually everyone who comes into contact with it? What stronger instrument of oppression is there than an increasingly aggressive IRS that has the power to presume people guilty until proven innocent? One way or another, every American can relate to a tax code that, as economist Herbert Stein put it, is full of "anomalies, distortions, and complexity." Perhaps tax reform could empower the people to rein in the welfare state and regain control over their government. Or at the very least, make life a little easier.

Each year Americans spend more than five billion hours complying with the tax code. Surely it wouldn't be difficult for any one of us to find a better way to spend our time. Moreover, three out of every five of us hire professional tax preparers. Yet, incredible as it might seem, that's not enough to satisfy the IRS. Each year, we are erroneously charged more than $5 billion in penalties.

At the same time, taxation has become so rampant that virtually everything that is made is taxed many times over. You have often heard the expression that "man cannot live by bread alone." With our tax code, this is literally true. Americans for Tax Reform's chief economist Peter Ferrara found that "in the process of production from the farm to the store, the government imposes about 30 taxes on a loaf of bread," which increases the cost of bread by about 35 cents a loaf, a most bitter flavor indeed.

While a number of these taxes are state and local taxes, excise taxes, or indirect taxes, the absurdity of how pervasive taxation has become is evident. Taxes are too widespread and they're too high. Worse still, these taxes run amok are taking a heavy toll on all Americans.

Taxes Imposed on Bread Production and Sales

Federal Corporate Income Taxes	Local Business Income Taxes
Federal Individual Income Taxes	Truck Excise Taxes
Federal Employee Payroll Taxes	Highway Tire Excise Tax
State Property Taxes	Federal Gasoline Excise Tax
Local Property Taxes	Diesel Fuel Excise Tax
State Corporate Income Taxes/Franchise Taxes	Use Tax for Heavy Highway Vehicles
State Individual Income Taxes	State Gasoline Tax
State General Corporate License Fees	State Motor Vehicle and Operator Licenses
Local Business License Fees/Franchise Taxes	State Public Highway User Taxes and Tolls
State Unemployment Compensation	Tire Disposal Fees
Energy Taxes	Oil Disposal Fees
Energy Environmental Surcharges	Environmental Impact Tax
State Telephone Taxes	State Wheat Farmer Check-Off Tax
General Telephone Service Excise Tax	State Sales Tax
Toll Telephone Service Excise Tax	Local Sales Tax

SOURCE: Peter Ferrara, Americans for Tax Reform

In the 1990s, until very recently, much was made of a slowdown in the growth of real after-tax middle-class incomes. Indeed, concern for the plight of the middle class became so acute that the phrase "middle-class income squeeze" was coined to describe the situation. Now, with more than six years of steady, strong economic growth, less attention is being focused on the middle class. The widespread assumption is that all is well, and most Americans are once more climbing the road to prosperity and happiness. But the facts tell a different story.

Taxes at all levels—from the federal income tax to local real estate levies—are the largest budget item for most middle-class families and the only one that it is virtually impossible for them to take action to reduce. Instead, every other item of the family budget, even necessities like food, clothing, and shelter, must give way.

By the early and middle 1990s, tax reform proposals—the flat tax and various forms of consumption taxes, which in some cases had been germinating for more than a decade—that went well beyond a mere tinkering or adjusting of the existing tax code grew in popularity. No longer was it sufficient to lower tax rates as in the 1980s. Only a dismantling of the mindlessly complex income tax code would do. Only then could taxpayers truly improve their lives. Only then could people be free to succeed in life.

By the beginning of 1998, there were at least three leading ideas for fundamental tax reform. Two of them proposed replacing the income tax with a consumption tax—though designed differently—and the third, a flat tax. Advocates of fundamental tax reform argue that the current tax code is broken beyond repair and should be replaced with either a National Retail Sales Tax or a Flat Tax. Simplification, tax relief, tax fairness, and increased personal saving and investment were the principal goals of all the would-be tax reformers.

National Retail Sales Tax: Legislation proposed by Congressman Dan Schaefer of Colorado (HR2001: The National Retail Sales Act of 1997) and sponsored by other representatives, including Ralph Hall (Texas), John Linder (Georgia), Billy Tauzin (Louisiana), and Sue Myrick (North Carolina), would replace the existing income tax with "a tax of 15 percent on the gross payments for the use, consumption or enjoyment in the United States of any taxable property or service, whether produced or rendered within or without the United States." All goods and services would be subject to this tax. This tax would generally be collected by businesses making sales to their customers and would be administered by the states with the states receiving a collection and remittance fee from the federal government. The IRS would be abolished. Dues, contributions, and other qualified payments to nonprofit organizations would remain tax exempt.

A Value-Added Tax (VAT): VATs are consumption taxes in which taxes are imposed on the value a business adds to a product. At present, no legislation has been introduced to replace the federal income tax with a VAT.

The shortcomings of the National Retail Sales Tax and the VAT are that they are regressive taxes. As such, the tax burden falls disproportionately on those having the lowest incomes.

The Flat Tax: The Flat Tax, or Single-Rate Tax, is currently the most popular tax reform proposal. To this effect, three pieces of flat tax legislation have been introduced. House Majority Leader Dick Armey (Texas), together with Alabama Senator Richard Shelby, introduced the Freedom and Fairness Restoration Act of 1997 (HR1040/S1040), which would replace the existing income tax with a 17 percent flat tax on personal and business income. This legislation would eliminate all deductions and maintain personal exemptions of $11,000 for individuals, $22,000 for married couples filing jointly, $11,400 for heads of household, and $5,000 per dependent. There would no longer be a marriage tax penalty. The tax would be levied on wage and pension income, but not interest, dividend, or capital gain income, as these other forms of income would already have been taxed at the corporate level.

★ ★ ★

GIVEN THE WIDESPREAD agreement that the current tax system is broken beyond repair and the growing public support for major tax reform, it is not surprising that there are a number of competing tax reform initiatives pending before the Congress. What is startling, at least on the surface, is that none of these proposals is likely even to make it out of committee for a full vote by either house of Congress. And when these proposals die at the end of the 105th Congress in January 1999, little public outcry is expected.

Astonishing? Hardly. The current tax reform proposals are curiously unsatisfying. While they offer major structural changes, tax relief, and in general a less oppressive tax collection bureaucracy, they do little to address the real issue at hand: government has gotten too big, too powerful, and too wasteful. People want more than tax relief. They want more than a friendlier tax collection system. They want more than easier-to-understand rules. What they want is to regain a measure of control of their own lives, their own destinies, which has been taken away from them as the government grows in power and scope. The people want an all-out attack on the leviathan that government has become. They want to address not just the revenue issue—a minor consideration—but government's basic role and the way it does business. Americans want tax relief that downsizes government. The National Tax Rebate does that.

The fundamental difference between the National Tax Rebate and the aforementioned tax reform measures is that the rebate downsizes government and provides tax relief. No competing plan offers similar value. No other plan does away with big government. Also, if combined with the other tax reform measures, it makes them work better. It eliminates concerns of regression and unfairness. It gives them a chance.

The National Tax Rebate would work well in a flat tax world and a consumption tax world. Best of all, it fits easily into our existing system. This makes it, perhaps, the most politically feasible of all the tax relief proposals. The National Tax Rebate is an idea that stands by itself. It is a bold new idea that is both economically and politically viable.

Today, we all too often hear politicians pledge middle-class tax relief. Then, when it happens—or at least when it's announced—the relief is so timid, so minuscule that everyone but the politicians needs a microscope to find it. Rather than promising middle-class tax relief, the National Tax Rebate provides it. And you don't need a magnifying glass to find it. You'll see it in your wallet.

The National Tax Rebate is a plan designed not around special interests and bureaucracy, but around the American family. It is a plan that downsizes Washington while upsizing the benefits we all get from our government. It's a plan that encourages work, productivity, and wealth creation, exactly the things that made this nation great. Finally, it's a plan that could become the biggest peacetime job creation program in our history.

The remainder of these pages will tell you everything you need to know about the National Tax Rebate, show you evidence it can work, provide real life examples that it has worked, and explain how you can regain your tax dollars from the government through the National Tax Rebate. It will show you how you can once more control your lives and create the future that you, not the government bureaucrats, want.

The way I see it, there is a silver lining to welfare's failure and the limitations of current reform efforts. It is that we now know what has not worked, and what cannot work. Considering that all the other attempts at reform have their shortcomings, you might think it will be difficult to build a policy around the framework I've outlined. Fortunately for us, this task is not difficult at all. It is readily available. It is the National Tax Rebate.

CHAPTER 3

Charting a New Course

"**THE REASON CONGRESS** had found it difficult to find a plan that provides universal benefits at a level regarded as reasonable, that preserves work incentives, and that is not vastly more expensive... is that no such plan exists or can be devised," Senior Fellow Henry Aaron of the Brookings Institution wrote twenty-five years ago. In a sense, he was right.

As long as government happily accepted the constraints of conventional thinking and refused to consider new, creative, and even unorthodox ideas, there could be no solution. As a mathematician, I know all too well that the same formula applied to the same problem will always yield same answer. Unless either the problem or the formula is changed, the solution remains the same.

Yet, even as the war on poverty began to fare worse and worse, and the economic and financial toll rose higher and higher, government refused to change its ways. Fueled by the sages of the status quo who retained their stranglehold over public policy, government occasionally tinkered with but otherwise remained devoted to its paternalistic ways.

All around them, though, the world was changing. Increasingly, the most successful companies were those that threw off the shackles of traditional industry thinking. They outright rejected the notion that industries made companies. Instead, they demonstrated that companies made industries. The most successful persons were no longer those who worked for Fortune 500 behemoths, but those who invented new things and started new businesses. Innovation and creativity became the order of the day, and the unconventional became the rule of thumb.

These successes notwithstanding, the Beltway gurus remained wedded to the status quo. They knew no other way. The prospect of change, however small, was just too frightening. Forget about big change. Had these devotees of the status quo held sway during the fifteenth, sixteenth, and seventeenth centuries, the world would still be flat, the sun would still revolve around the earth, we would still live by candlelight, we would still travel by horse-drawn carriage, and mercantilism would still be our economic foundation. Where would we be then?

Sadly, for us taxpayers and the poor persons government was supposed to liberate from poverty, conventional inside-the-Beltway thinking ensured that government's guiding assumption remained "[you name the idea] could not be done." And little was done.

THE NATIONAL TAX REBATE would throw the now discredited conventional inside-the-Beltway logic out the window. It would turn the status quo on its head.

The National Tax Rebate would cash out the myriad, costly government assistance programs and replace them with a simple, universal cash grant of $1,000 a month for every American family of four. All said, it would give $720 billion dollars of our money back to us!

The National Tax Rebate is an unparalleled opportunity creation grant. In one blow, it would substantially eliminate government waste, emasculate government bureaucracy, and empower the people. Once more, individuals and families, not government bureaucrats, would decide how best to meet their unique needs. People would again live their lives, not as the government or its legion of bureaucrats saw fit, but in the manner they chose. They would no longer be punished with excessive effective marginal tax rates for seeking to better their lives and those of their families.

Sound radical? It probably does. But that is only because we have become accustomed to government bureaucrats making an increasing number of decisions for us. We have learned to defer to their judgment. We have forgotten what it is like to be fully free, to make our own decisions, to shape our own destinies.

The rise of the welfare state is a recent phenomenon. It is not an immutable reality. There was a time in which government was not so big or paternalistic. Now, in the welfare state's failure—a very costly one at that—we find the seeds of opportunity. We have a chance to build a society in which the individual matters most. We have a chance to replace the safety net and its poverty trap with a society of opportunity in which there are no limits on what you might achieve. "There are no limits on our future if we don't put limits on our people," Jack Kemp remarked. That is the kind of society my National Tax Rebate seeks to create.

Wouldn't you like just such a society, one in which you are free to fulfill your full potential? I've lived that kind of life—in that era. With today's paralyzing welfare state, I would never have accomplished what I did. I want you to have the same opportunities I had. With the National Tax Rebate, I truly believe that you would have at least the same chance to make a difference as I had, maybe better.

Today, you often hear that there is no room for simple principles in our immensely complicated world. Nothing is permanent; everything is relative. What is here today is gone tomorrow. I disagree. Such a world precludes the possibility of human nature. There are principles that have survived the test of time. These are the principles upon which our democratic society has been created, upon which man has always gotten ahead.

The National Tax Rebate is founded on six simple but powerful principles:

1. every person is motivated by self-interest and, therefore, responds to incentives

2. each person can be trusted, on average, to make good decisions

3. work is essential to personal well-being

4. people learn from experience

5. targeted, one-size-fits-all government solutions cannot succeed

6. it's our money, anyway.

People are motivated by self-interest and respond to incentives: We are all rational beings who act in our own best interests. We continually strive to better our situations, enrich our lives, and take advantage of our opportunities. We work hard, not for work's sake, but because it will improve our lives. We respond to incentives. Wherever there is the prospect of gain, so long as it does not involve compromising our most basic values or put us at excessive risk, we respond. That is human nature. Despite all the changes that have taken place since the emergence of man, human nature has barely changed.

Our entire free enterprise system is built on incentives. Indeed, there is no better mirror image of human nature than the market system at work. Incentives alone are the reason the market system has proved superior to every other alternative. Businesses that provide quality products and services at an affordable price are rewarded with profit and growth. Those that don't are punished by losses and inevitable failure. What's more, people can keep the rewards of their labor. They can use these rewards, be they cash or shares of stock, to improve their standard of living. This concept of ownership provides a compelling reason for people to succeed. The system encourages, rewards, and reinforces success. And success begets success. Is there any mystery as to why our economy has become so strong or created so much wealth?

Unfortunately, our government is baffled by what should be obvious. It still assumes that man, unlike all other animals, is willing to work without incentives. Thus, government created a welfare system that, in many cases, made public assistance more lucrative than work, and punished efforts to escape public dependency. In the end, only the government seemed surprised by the outcome when poverty prevailed.

The National Tax Rebate would change all this. In no case would public assistance be more attractive than work—because there would be no welfare system. Furthermore, the exorbitant effective marginal tax rates imposed on those starting work would be but a bad memory. People would be encouraged to work. They would be rewarded for working. And without doubt, they would overwhelmingly choose to work.

People make good decisions: Our nation's Founding Fathers based the entire American experiment on the notion that the average person could be trusted to make good decisions. Nobody expected every person to make perfect decisions, just good ones. "If the ordinary Joe did nothing more than make an honest living and take care of his family, he was as good an American as the highest in the land," Charles Murray observed. Economist Ludwig von Mises wrote, "The common man is supreme in the market economy. He is the customer who 'is always right.'" Besides, when it comes to spending money, we will always make better decisions than the bureaucrats. We spend our own money. They spend other peoples' money.

Our nation's Founders assumed that virtually every person was capable of taking care of himself, and they carefully crafted a constitution that guaranteed their basic freedoms, specifically enumerated the federal government's powers, and left all other areas on which the Constitution was silent to the states and people. That this once-heretical concept of self-government not only has survived for more than two hundred years, but has also become the preferred model worldwide is confirmation that our Founding Fathers' faith in the ordinary person was well placed. After all, if the average person was incapable of taking care of himself, he would be equally incapable of handling his civic responsibilities. In that case, no representative government could survive for long.

History has validated our Founders' wisdom. "[T]he genius of the American system is that through freedom we have created extraordinary results from plain old ordinary people," Senator Phil Gramm commented.

The National Tax Rebate would return decision-making power to the people. They would make their own choices over virtually every aspect of their lives, so long as their choices would not interfere with the lives and choices of others.

Work is essential to personal well-being: There is no better vehicle for raising one's standard of living than work. Work provides the skills, experience, and knowledge essential to personal success. Entry level jobs provide meaningful job training for future career advancement in a way no government program ever could.

In America "there is a tendency to denigrate 'hamburger flipping'...," Irwin Stelzer of the American Enterprise Institute states. "This is wrong on all counts.... Any entry-level job teaches the important skills of showing up for work, regularly and on time, suitably clothed and prepared to cooperate with other workers and to attempt to please customers. These are vital skills."

And Ben Wildavsky, Staff Correspondent, *National*

Journal, wrote that "McDonald's has been a frequent target for those expounding the 'dead-end jobs' thesis.... While the typical complaints... certainly have some basis in reality... a surprising number of burger flippers advance through the ranks and enjoy the benefits that go with managerial responsibility in a demanding business. More important, most employees who pass through McDonald's gain the kinds of skills that help them get better jobs." And, his coup de grâce: "Far from sticking its workers in an inescapable rut, McDonald's functions as a de facto job training program by teaching the basics of how to work."

By any stretch of the imagination, entry-level work is not dead-end work. It is the first rung on the ladder of opportunity.

Unfortunately for those who would most benefit from entry-level work, the wages these positions pay are often difficult if not impossible to live on, particularly for large families. The National Tax Rebate would demolish this barrier to opportunity by lifting every person onto the first rung of the ladder. When combined with the National Tax Rebate, every wage would be a livable wage. Every person would be able to take advantage of the workplace's rich possibilities.

People learn from experience: People learn most from doing things. They gain most from trying new things. The National Tax Rebate would provide the financial means to take some risks, for example to launch that start-up business they could only dream about. Not everybody would succeed in their entrepreneurial pursuits, but everybody who tried would gain from the experience.

They would learn more about themselves, their interests, and their capabilities. This new knowledge would allow them to better focus their efforts on those activities from which they would have the most to gain.

"One of the key moral hazards entailed in government job programs and other insurance schemes is the loss of knowledge—a real capital loss—that they inflict on citizens who never learn their own best abilities and opportunities," George Gilder observed in *Wealth & Poverty*. The National Tax Rebate would be an avenue to this knowledge; it would be a real capital gain. Everyone would benefit directly or indirectly.

Targeted, one-size-fits-all government solutions are recipes for failure: Every person's and family's needs are uniquely different. No one person's or family's circumstances are identical. Neither are any person's or family's aspirations. By applying a one-size-fits-all policy to those it seeks to help, government is wasting resources that could be used far more effectively and efficiently with a more flexible approach. At best, the government's current strategy is sheer folly. At worst, it is outright arrogance.

By providing each person with cash, the National Tax Rebate offers a customized solution that fits every person's particular needs and circumstances. By and large, as mentioned earlier, no one can make better decisions on how to spend money than the person himself. Consequently, the National Tax Rebate would offer more purchasing power to those who would most benefit than would be possible from any in-kind assistance program.

Targeting is inherently discriminatory. Either you qualify or you don't. Those who qualify stand to gain.

Those who don't, lose. Even those who gain, though, often do so at the price of being labeled failures, or worse. Think of all the negative connotations associated with welfare. An enlightened nation like ours deserves better. Much better.

The National Tax Rebate would not discriminate. Every person regardless of age, race, income, or any variable of your choice would qualify. The benefit would be universal; there would be no artificial, if not perverted, thresholds; no more "haves" versus "have nots." No longer would petty envy cripple our nation's effort to eradicate poverty. Everyone would be treated alike. Now that is true fairness.

It's our money: Government has no money of its own. It uses our tax dollars. The National Tax Rebate would not be a reduction in the government's assets; it would be a refund of our money.

Given government's demonstrated ability to mismanage our money, we deserve to regain control over our funds. We work hard day after day, week after week, month after month, all year long for our wages. Government takes two out of every five dollars we earn. We have a right to demand that it use our resources wisely. The government owes us accountability. Put another way, it is simply wrong for the government to continue to misspend our hard-earned dollars when we could do a far better job.

The National Tax Rebate would refund a substantial portion of our tax dollars and return the decision-making to us. We would do the rest. And make no mistake about it, the results would be breathtaking.

THE NATIONAL TAX REBATE would provide enormous social and economic benefits. But there is one big problem. It's a pie-in-the-sky scheme that would blow a gaping hole in the federal budget. It would bring an abrupt end to the dawning era of federal budget surpluses. Right? Wrong!

In one of the most remarkable findings ever made at the Institute for SocioEconomic Studies (ISES), it was discovered that full funding is already available. We don't need a tax increase. Besides, a tax hike would undercut the tax relief aimed at in the National Tax Rebate. Therefore, the National Tax Rebate would not be financed by raising taxes. Neither would there be new government spending. Not one cent. The National Tax Rebate would preserve the budgetary gains that have put the federal government back on the road to budget surpluses. Our government is already spending all the money needed every single year. And it is spending this money, albeit very poorly, for exactly the same purpose the Rebate would have, namely to make some financial assistance available to Americans.

In 1977 our researchers, working with Pace University, found 182 federal programs geared to providing income support for Americans. Today, according to *The 1997 Catalog of Federal Domestic Assistance*, that number exceeds one thousand. But what about the dollars? These programs have expenditures that total more than $720 billion each year. That's huge! Refunding this money to the people would result in a tax cut of a magnitude unrivaled in history.

By relying solely on funds raised from cashing out existing spending programs, fiscal hawks could be assured that the National Tax Rebate would have no adverse budgetary impact. Proponents of tax relief could celebrate the unprecedented tax cuts it would bring. Who says you can't cut taxes and keep the budget balanced all at the same time? The National Tax Rebate would do both! And as an added bonus, it would afford the government the luxury of using its surpluses to pay down its more than $5 trillion debt.

What the National Tax Rebate would not do, however, is eliminate government. All vital government programs would be left intact. National defense spending, Social Security, Medicare, interest on the federal debt, to name a few, would all be untouched.

What the National Tax Rebate would do is make the government work better than ever before. The people would spend the rebate money as they see fit. And government would concentrate on its core functions. Focused government would stand a real chance of becoming excellent government. It certainly would be far more effective than today's government, which seeks to do everything for everybody all the time, but only does everything poorly all the time. At long last, the quality revolution that has been transforming corporate America into powerhouse competitors for the last twenty years would reach the steps of Washington. Finally, our government, once an institution that inspired only pride, would begin to earn back its lost luster.

THE NATIONAL TAX REBATE certainly seems appealing. Sufficient funding is readily available. And it would empower the people. It would restore accountable government. It would preserve fiscal responsibility while providing serious tax relief. These are all popular causes. Who wouldn't want to bring more power to the people, see the government become more accountable, cut taxes, and balance the budget all at the same time?

Nonetheless, we wanted to explore all the options. We wanted to examine all the alternatives that could do what the National Tax Rebate seeks to do, only better. After all, the change this book is advancing would be truly revolutionary. We had to be sure that this concept would hold together under rigorous academic scrutiny.

To look into the matter, the ISES commissioned Columbia University's School of Social Work to conduct a comprehensive analysis of a wide range of options for their impact on poverty, as well as their feasibility. The study lasted one year and entailed the creation of an original dynamic microsimulation to model the effects of the alternatives being evaluated. It utilized data from the March 1995 Current Population Survey (CPS) database (a monthly cross-sectional survey of a large sample of the U.S. population conducted by the U.S. Bureau of the Census), administrative data recorded in *The 1993 Green Book*, and *The 1995 Catalog of Federal Domestic Assistance*.

Finally, the results came in. They confirmed our most hopeful expectations. The National Tax Rebate would benefit most Americans even though a substantial number of government programs would be eliminated. It would also virtually eliminate poverty when combined with the income earned from even a part-time job. A carefully designed National Tax Rebate could restore the incentive to work and give Americans what they most need from the government: meaningful financial help (tax relief) without crippling restrictions and wasteful bureaucracy. With the National Tax Rebate we would not have to worry about ending welfare as we know it. We could end welfare of any kind, period.

Permanently end welfare? That's right. The Columbia study stated that the National Tax Rebate could be designed to provide the middle class with real tax relief, while accomplishing the ultimate in welfare reform: making welfare completely unnecessary.

"Tax rebates decrease poverty more effectively than the current system…," the study declared. "Tax rebates can reduce both government and poverty and provide meaningful middle-class tax relief."

"All five tax rebate plans reduced the aggregate poverty rate and the aggregate poverty gap," it added. "This is true no matter which assumption is made about the value of in-kind benefits to recipients." Estimates on the loss in value resulting from the inefficiency of in-kind benefits range from 10 percent to 25 percent of their gross value.

How about the numbers? Under a National Tax Rebate, depending on its design, the poverty rate for all persons would fall to somewhere between 1.75 percent and 7.83 percent. In other words, the poverty rate would fall by more than 40 percent. Perhaps it could fall by more than 80 percent. The poverty rate for children would fall almost as significantly to between 2.05 percent and 13.47 percent. Finally, the poverty rate for the elderly would range between 0 percent and 7.03 percent.

The poverty gap—the amount of additional money needed for all persons to raise themselves above the poverty threshold—would shrink from today's $40 billion to as low as $7.97 billion. And these findings take into consideration that people might not be more inclined to work even as welfare is abolished, a most unlikely scenario.

"But those were largely 1995 numbers, and this is 1998!" you might protest. "Besides, the minimum wage was much lower then."

Fair enough. Let's advance the calendar to today. Once we do that, the figures are equally impressive. Indeed, when combined with even a half-time minimum wage job, every person would be raised above the poverty threshold.

"But what if people don't work?"

That's their choice. The National Tax Rebate is not about making work unnecessary. It's about making poverty unknown for those who work. No longer would there be any excuse for people to forego work. There would be no fallback to subsidized idleness. Of course, the widely familiar myth that welfare recipients are lazy and prefer not to work is just that, a bad myth. But by making welfare as generous as it is, government made public assistance preferable. And because people look after their own best interests, the outcome—dependency—could not be any less surprising. Still, why take the chance? The National Tax Rebate would make work a necessity for overcoming poverty.

★ ★ ★

THIS LOOKS GREAT! Minimum wage work, even half-time minimum wage work, when combined with the National Tax Rebate would lift everyone out of poverty. That's the point. The objective, unlike that of the existing welfare system, is to encourage people to work. To give them an incentive to work. Is life without poverty a powerful enough incentive? I certainly think so. People would be highly motivated to take entry-level work. And

Impact of the National Tax Rebate and a Full-Time Minimum Wage Income ($4,000 rebate for adults; $2,000 rebate for children)				
Family Size	Poverty Threshold (annual)	Value of Tax Rebate (annual)	Full-Time Minimum Wage (annual)	Combined Income as a % of Poverty Threshold
1	$8,178	$4,000	$10,300	175%
2	$10,468	$8,000	$10,300	175%
3	$12,803	$10,000	$10,300	159%
4	$16,404	$12,000	$10,300	136%

Impact of the National Tax Rebate and a Half-Time Minimum Wage Income ($4,000 rebate for adults; $2,000 rebate for children)				
Family Size	Poverty Threshold (annual)	Value of Tax Rebate (annual)	Full-Time Minimum Wage (annual)	Combined Income as a % of Poverty Threshold
1	$8,178	$4,000	$5,150	112%
2	$10,468	$8,000	$5,150	126%
3	$12,803	$10,000	$5,150	118%
4	$16,404	$12,000	$5,150	105%

it would be to every person's financial advantage to do the things necessary for career advancement. The ultimate reward would be a satisfactory standard of living, or at least a life without poverty.

The National Tax Rebate would substantially reduce poverty with no new government programs or spending. Better still, it would substantially reduce poverty at the same time the middle class was receiving significant tax relief. No government program could make a similar claim. As history has shown, nothing has ever been able to do what the National Tax Rebate could.

★ ★ ★

EVEN AS THE ACADEMIC evidence strongly supports the potential positive impact of a National Tax Rebate, a number of important objections need to be addressed.

Perhaps the biggest objection is that it would reduce work incentives for low-income earners.

"The National Tax Rebate is a form of guaranteed income," the argument goes. "Guaranteed incomes reduce the need to work, because more income allows people to partake of more leisure."

A strong argument. Few would disagree that higher incomes allow people more leisure and less work.

But the National Tax Rebate is no ordinary guaranteed income scheme. It is a multifaceted approach that includes eliminating the current welfare system in exchange for cash. By doing so, it eliminates the ability of people to receive more in public assistance than from working. It eliminates the impenetrable barriers that currently stand between welfare and work. It annihilates the 100 percent or more effective marginal tax rates that flatten the hopes and aspirations of those who seek to free themselves from the welfare trap.

Most important, the National Tax Rebate alone does not bring you out of poverty. Instead, to rise above poverty, you must work. There is no way around it.

Now if people choose not to work, they would also be choosing not to escape poverty. With the National Tax Rebate, poverty would be a voluntary choice. Given that we all make decisions that are in our own best interest, I highly doubt that many would purposely degrade their standard of living just to avoid work. On the contrary, virtually everyone would embrace work, regardless of the wage offered. In the end, everyone would be better for it as they began to climb America's ladder of opportunity.

In addition, a number of important academic studies have shown that replacing in-kind benefits with cash would not reduce work incentives for low-income earners. Between 1969 and 1971, the University of Wisconsin's Institute for Research into Poverty along with Mathematica Policy Research administered four pilot projects to investigate the empirical effects of replacing in-kind benefits with cash on low-income earners.

Then in 1975, the Brookings Institution hosted a conference that brought together a number of nationally known economists to discuss their analyses of the pilot projects. They determined that the fear that replacing in-kind benefits with cash would undermine work incentives for low-income earners was largely unfounded. A study of lottery winners by Dr. H. Roy Kaplan of the Florida Institute of Technology lent additional support to this finding. Indeed, the project showed that this approach actually increased work incentives for some low-income groups while having no demonstrated adverse impact on the others. Employment increased among African Americans and Hispanics, two groups that have historically suffered from disproportionately high rates of joblessness.

Finally, the behavior of lottery winners, which will be discussed later, provides conclusive evidence that a National Tax Rebate would not undermine work incentives. If anything, it would enhance people's incentive to work.

Another potent objection involves cutting and flattening tax rates.

"Why not cash out these programs and reduce tax rates?"

Another good question. Tax relief always makes good sense. High taxes discourage work. They discourage risk-taking entrepreneurship. They diminish every aspect of our standard of living. Worst of all, they impair our future well-being—all of our hopes, all of our dreams. Cutting tax rates would certainly help. Flattening tax rates, which in effect would reduce the excise tax on hard work and success inherent in the existing multirate system, would also help. But we could do more with a National Tax Rate. Far more.

The National Tax Rebate would provide much more "bang for the buck." It would not just furnish ample tax relief, but also virtually eliminate poverty. Reduced tax rates would merely benefit existing taxpayers. The National Tax Rebate would benefit existing taxpayers and future taxpayers—everyone would have an incentive to work.

Lowering tax rates would do little to alleviate the plight of low-income or poverty-stricken individuals who currently don't have incomes sufficient to pay taxes. The rebate approach would have a huge impact on those individuals and families, putting them into a strong position to take advantage of the opportunities available to them. It would make even part-time minimum wage jobs livable. It would make entry-level work highly appealing while eliminating the welfare system's countless incentives not to work. People motivated to seek work, to take entry-level positions, would gain both the skills and work experience essential to better-paying, more advanced positions. In time, it would transform them into taxpayers. The broadening of our tax base could then lead to even lower tax rates in the future.

"But our income tax system is highly inefficient and wasteful," you might counter. "Doesn't the National Tax Rebate lock this system into place?"

It wouldn't. The National Tax Rebate is sufficiently flexible that it could easily fit with the current system or any one of the alternatives being advanced. The National Tax Rebate is a fundamental change in the way government does business. How it raises revenue has little bearing on how it operates. The nation needs more than just tax relief. It needs more than just welfare reform. It needs a fresh new approach that would put the people back in charge. The National Tax Rebate would provide considerable tax relief while simultaneously returning decision-making to the people, something that no other singular reform could attempt.

"This sounds great!" you might exclaim. "Maybe we should try the rebate, perhaps a partial one, in a few states to see how it would work."

No. In this case, prudence would be recklessness. A go-slow, piecemeal approach could mortally compromise the concept. The impact of a National Tax Rebate-lite might be too small to make a noticeable difference. Then, the champions of the status quo would point to its limited impact as proof that it could not work. And hope for eliminating poverty would be frozen in time.

How can that be? As a rule of thumb, you should proceed slowly. Otherwise, you could get more than you bargained for. The results could be ruinous.

Once again, that's the conventional wisdom the pundits of impossibility love to convey. Private sector experience has demonstrated over and over again that big change should be implemented quickly. The corporate restructuring efforts that have failed most often have been those that were attempted over too long a period of time or were too incremental in scope. Those that were most successful were quick and decisive. The same would hold true for the National Tax Rebate. Big change requires big action, quickly. Time is the best ally opponents of change can have. Unless the forces of the status quo are kept off balance—better yet, swept away—their triumph is assured.

The objections addressed here are just the principal ones that could be raised. There are many more minor ones. But as a general rule—and here's one that has been proven right time and time again—if the viability and practicality of the National Tax Rebate are challenged, ask the challenger to find a better alternative. And if there is a better solution, where is it, and why hasn't the welfare state been replaced by it?

The time has come to shut down our failed welfare experiment. We know the outcome. It has not worked, and it cannot work. Russell Roberts of Washington University in St. Louis, noting the absurdity of our existing welfare system, eloquently declared, "The only way to avoid national indigestion is to close the government restaurant where few benefit at the expense of many." Each year on April 15, we suffer that indigestion when we see our slimmed-down wallets and the gluttonous welfare state that devoured our hard-earned wages. Each year this indigestion grows worse.

No doubt about it. The National Tax Rebate is a revolutionary concept. It would bring sweeping change for the better. Those who wish to preserve the existing system, and that includes those who peddle tiny solutions for our nation's big challenges, have already had their shot. They've failed—*miserably*. We're $5 trillion poorer for it; more than one out of every ten persons is in poverty for it. The burden of proof isn't on us. The burden of failure is on them.

CHAPTER 4

The National Tax Rebate Tested

"THE FACTS WILL EVENTUALLY test all our theories and they form... the only impartial jury to which we can appeal," Jean Louis Randolphe Agassiz wrote in *Geological Studies*. That was more than a century ago. His keen observation is as true today as it was then, and it will be as applicable tomorrow.

One often hears of the brilliant theory that disintegrated when exposed to reality. It was so original. It was so logical. Indeed, it was perfect.

All the analysis, all the research, everything that was done only supported and strengthened the theory. Yet, it fell apart so quickly when unveiled in the real world. It never had a chance. Its concept—and a remarkable one it was!——could not bridge the treacherous chasm between fragile hypothesis and hard fact.

The moral of this story is all too clear. What happens in the world of abstract theory matters little. What happens in the world of reality, the world in which we live and interact every day of our lives, is the only thing that matters. Sure, historians may remember the past's biggest setbacks and most dramatic falls. But what's most memorable are its successes. It's the successes, layer upon layer of them, on which we proceed. It's from these foundations that we spring ahead.

Everything we have seen to date indicates that the National Tax Rebate works—Columbia University's microsimulation, evidence from past experiments in which in-kind assistance was replaced with cash, the debris of our failed welfare state, and the immense power of our market economy at work.

People respond to incentives. People do best when they have the freedom to make the choices that most appropriately address their unique needs and most effectively propel them toward their distinct hopes and aspirations. People soar to their greatest heights when they have the resources to take risks, try new things, fire their imaginations. The National Tax Rebate would provide the incentives, decision-making power, and resources to bring out the best from every American family and individual. Or at least, that's the theory of it. And it definitely looks good on paper.

But what about the real world, the only place that really matters? Can the National Tax Rebate live up to its advertised billing?

The answer is a resounding yes! It already has.

From the lottery to the Alaskan dividend to the Earned Income Tax Credit (EITC), we have glimpsed its awesome potential. We have seen that it can and does work well. We have seen that personal decision-making is vastly superior to bureaucratic meddling. All of this has already happened in the sunlight of the real world.

In short: The rebate concept has been tried in various

forms and shapes. It has worked. And people are happy with the results.

★ ★ ★

YOUR SPOUSE AND YOU are seated on the sofa directly in front of your television. During a commercial break, the winning lottery numbers are being drawn. You have your ticket, but you are not expecting much—no one you know has ever won—and you halfheartedly check your numbers as the drawing commences.

"The first number is 10, the next is 25, and the next…," the attractive young woman standing in the foreground of your television screen calls out.

You become excited. You have the first three numbers.

"And the final number is 7."

You're in a state of shock. All of the numbers called match the numbers you picked.

"This can't be happening!" you exclaim under your breath. Your spouse says that yes, you have indeed won.

In a few days, you will be a millionaire several times over. You will travel around the world. You will quit your job and retire to a life of luxury. Right?

Not exactly. The National Tax Rebate is not a lottery. But I use this example to illustrate that when people come into large sums of money, amounts similar to what the rebate would provide, they do not quit work or waste the money on frivolous things. Contrary to what you might expect, the lives of lottery winners remain much the same as before luck smiled on them. They remain at their work, for example. Indeed, from their daily itinerary you could hardly tell that they had won the lottery.

But how is the lottery pertinent to the National Tax Rebate? One is based on mere chance, the other on political will. Actually, the experiences of lottery winners, the choices they make, and the things they do after winning the lottery are highly relevant.

One of the most valuable real-life tools for examining the likely effects of the National Tax Rebate is the impact winning the lottery has had on its winners. A comprehensive study of lottery winners conducted by Professor Dr. H. Roy Kaplan of the Florida Institute for Technology on behalf of the Institute for SocioEconomic Studies in 1984 provided convincing evidence that the extra income afforded by the National Tax Rebate would have no adverse impact on people's work habits.

Professor Kaplan, author of *Lottery Winners: How They Won and How Winning Changed Their Lives* and a leading authority on the topic, found that winning the lottery had no negative effect on the work behavior of the lottery winners. A recent examination of the experience of thirty-nine lottery winners in Roby, Texas, strongly supported Dr. Kaplan's findings.

The lottery study is a good proxy for the National Tax Rebate for four important reasons. First, the evidence is based not on what people said that they would do, but on what they did. The study deals with actual human behavior, not intended behavior. Second, all of the lottery winners received regular payments for a prolonged period of time. None of them received lump sum payments. In the case of the lottery study, each lottery winner received an annual payment. Third, a substantial number of lottery winners received payments of $10,000 or less per year—

amounts well within the range of the National Tax Rebate. Finally, the lottery study is useful because the lottery winners are representative of the nation's population as a whole. The winners were randomly determined (lottery numbers are randomly selected) and came from every background. The only thing special about the lottery winners is that they won their lotteries. Otherwise, they are just like the rest of us. Consequently, the impact that winning the lottery had on their lives and activities is a particularly good model of the impact a National Tax Rebate would have on its recipients: the American people.

Kaplan's study was based on the data of 976 people (576 lottery winners and 400 spouses). The winners received amounts ranging from less than $50,000 to be paid over twenty years to more than $2 million payable over the same time frame.

The study showed that winning the lottery resulted in no significant behavioral changes for the overwhelming majority of winners.

"Only 11 percent (49) of the winners and 13 percent (34) of the spouses quit their jobs during the first year after winning, out of a total of 446 winners and 253 spouses who were employed at the time they won," observed Kaplan. "The number of people who changed their work behavior (i.e., quit, retired, reduced hours, and changed jobs) increased as the size of the winnings increased. Over and above the size of the prize, work decisions were influenced by age, marital status, occupation, length of employment, hours worked, and education.... [T]he vast majority of winners and their spouses kept working."

Even more revealing was the fact that virtually no winners receiving less than $10,000 annually left the workforce. Only 5 percent quit their jobs. This change is little different from the background changes taking place in the labor force due to frictional (people temporarily between jobs) and structural (people leaving the workforce due to a mismatch between their skills and labor needs) unemployment. Of those leaving their jobs, most either did so to retire (they were primarily aged sixty-five and above and would likely have retired anyway) or to spend more time with their children. In fact, 18 percent of winners and 35 percent of spouses reduced their work activity solely to spend additional time caring for their children. Winning the lottery enabled forty-four winners to go back to school to further their educations, and allowed fifty-nine others to make career changes. In almost every case, people's changed work habits had everything to do with either their personal self-improvement or improving the quality of life of their families. It had nothing to do with leaving work for the sake of not working. So much for the stereotypical lazy lottery winner.

Other important findings included: winners holding skilled or professional positions were more likely to retain their jobs; those having more years of schooling were also more likely to remain at their jobs; those with higher incomes prior to their lottery windfall were more likely to stay at their jobs; and married winners were also more likely to continue their jobs. This is exactly what most socioeconomic studies would have predicted.

Now that more than a decade has passed since

Kaplan's study, perhaps people have changed the way they would react to similar winnings. Maybe the data are obsolete and should no longer be relied upon? No. Although the calendar has changed, people have not. The experience of the thirty-nine winners in Roby, Texas, who won more than $1 million each, refuted any thought that people's behavior today is radically different from when Kaplan conducted his seminal study. Why should it be? Human nature has changed little if at all since man's emergence.

The year 1996 was a great year for a group of thirty-nine people in Roby, a small town in western Texas with a population of roughly 250 people. It was a year they would never forget. This group had been pooling their lottery tickets for some time. Then in 1996, they won the big prize. Each one of the group won more than a million dollars. Now, for the next forty years, each of the winners receives just under $40,000 a year after taxes. Certainly with that kind of additional income, luxury cars, jewels, fur coats, and caviar must abound. They don't.

Instead, the mundane prevails. Roby's lottery winners used their unexpected bonanza to reduce their personal debts—a home mortgage here, a credit card balance there—establish savings accounts for their children's education, purchase health insurance, and in one case, to create an investment pool to help finance the construction of a new cottonseed-oil plant. With regard to their careers, hard work remains the name of the game. This is hardly the stuff dreams are made of.

This startling evidence from the experience of the two

sets of lottery winners—that few lottery winners either quit their jobs or substantially altered their work habits—refutes perhaps the most potent argument against the National Tax Rebate, namely, that such a rebate would create a strong work disincentive.

While it is easy for academics to cite elaborate models or simulations of human behavior to promote their assertions, most of these models fall far short of appreciating the complexity of real-life human decision-making. Most of these models tend to be simplistic representations that crumble, not unlike the story of the failed theory at the beginning of this chapter, when exposed to the real world. They are merely models in search of something to represent.

But the lottery results have nothing to do with mere theory and everything to do with actual experience. And actual experience is the only thing that truly matters. Even more important from the vantage point of being able to predict the impact a National Tax Rebate would have on people's work habits, the lottery results are consistent over time and place.

Winning the lottery "has made my job easier.... I feel that my goals before winning should remain the same," a winner of $1.3 million told Dr. Kaplan. These comments were not the exception. They were typical. People's activities are more the product of their basic values and outlook in life than changes in income. Income fluctuates; deeply held values don't. Money can enable you more easily to achieve your desired lifestyle, but it cannot create it. Not surprisingly, a lottery winner's lifestyle and work habits usually changed little or not at all.

At first glance, these results seem more than a little surprising. They shouldn't be. In reality, the argument that lottery winnings would change people's lives beyond recognition and shatter their incentive to work is ridiculous. If the argument that lottery winnings undermined people's work incentives were true, it would be extremely hazardous for employers to give their top producers raises or bonuses. Doing so, after all, would impair the productivity of their top performers.

Based on these practical data, there is little doubt that a National Tax Rebate would qualitatively improve people's lives without reducing their incentive to work.

★　★　★

ALL RIGHT, THE LOTTERY winners kept on working even after becoming millionaires. But low-income earners are said to be different. The minute they come into extra money—cash—they would cut their work hours and increase their leisure time. In other words, they would commit economic suicide. Thus it is too risky to give them cash.

That is the thought behind in-kind assistance programs. The poor cannot be trusted to take care of themselves. Government must do it for them.

Actual experience shows otherwise. The poor, just like everybody else, can take care of themselves. They can and do act responsibly, even heroically in the face of harsh circumstances made worse by the government's many penalties for upward mobility.

Evidence from a May 1997 General Accounting

Office (GAO) report on the Earned Income Tax Credit (EITC) program—a cash subsidy that is administered to low-income workers through the tax code—reveals that more persons who receive the EITC experience rising incomes than falling incomes. Even more remarkable, they raise their incomes even as they face a stiff built-in penalty for doing so. The way the EITC is designed, your EITC falls and then disappears the more you raise your income. This is not exactly the way to reward low-income persons who seek to better their fortunes. It's yet another poverty trap that ensnares our most unfortunate citizens.

Martin Anderson, former senior economic adviser to President Reagan, writes, "A person's desire for additional income is unquestionably diminished when he realizes that he can keep only half or one-fourth of it for himself." That is what the EITC and the rest of the welfare system do. Even then, the EITC penalty has not stopped low-income earners from raising their incomes.

The GAO report tracked the Earned Income Tax Credit participation and income for 27.3 million taxpayers who claimed the EITC for families with children at least once between tax year 1990 and 1995. These taxpayers filed a total of sixty-nine million claims for a total of $73 billion.

Two major trends manifested themselves. First, EITC recipients slowly graduated from the EITC. Second, in spite of heavy financial incentives not to increase their incomes, more EITC recipients raised their earnings than lowered them.

Between 1990 and 1995, 68 percent of EITC participants claimed the EITC at least two of the five years; 46 percent claimed it at least three of five years; 29 percent claimed it at least four years; and 16 percent claimed it all five years. In terms of consecutive years, 73 percent claimed the EITC for two or more consecutive years; 56 percent claimed it for three or more consecutive years; 44 percent claimed it four or more consecutive years; and 36 percent claimed it five consecutive years.

During the same period of time, 25 percent of EITC participants reported a higher income one year after claiming the EITC and 21 percent reported a falling income. Two years after a claim, 30 percent had a higher income and 26 percent a lower income. Three years after a claim, 32 percent had a higher income and 28 percent a lower income. Finally, four years after a claim, 36 percent had a higher income versus 29 percent with a lower income. Even more impressive, the number of claimants becoming ineligible for the EITC due to having an income above the EITC threshold rose from 10 percent one year after claiming the EITC to 18 percent four years after an EITC claim. Such upward mobility is not the behavior expected from lazy individuals seeking a free ride.

The poor, like everyone else, aspire to a better lifestyle. And they are willing to pay a severe price in order to achieve that better life. Given the sacrifices low-income earners are willing to endure along the road to upward mobility, there is little or no likelihood that the National Tax Rebate would undercut their incentive to work. The American people's desire for a higher standard of living is too strong.

THE LOTTERY STUDIES and experience from the EITC are good approximations of how people would respond to the National Tax Rebate. Based on the cumulative evidence, it seems more likely than not that the National Tax Rebate would not discourage work, and that low-income earners who would stand the most to gain from continued work would remain in the workforce.

Still, these studies are only representations. They are not actual tax rebates. Consequently, a few may still harbor some doubts.

"Forget the lottery, forget the EITC, how about the Rebate?" a skeptic might persist. "Will the real thing really work as intended?"

OK, how about the Rebate? Let's take a look at the Rebate itself!

"But how can this be? There's no such thing!"

On the weight of the evidence, there seems little chance of addressing the doubters' last misgiving. Given that the National Tax Rebate is far from law—there is not a single piece of legislation pending either before the Congress or any one of the state legislatures that would bring the National Tax Rebate to fruition—the skeptics' challenge appears insurmountable. How could you possibly know what the real thing would do unless it's in place? Well, we have to look no further than our northernmost state, Alaska, and its residents for the answer.

Two decades ago, Governor Jay Hammond of Alaska signed historic legislation granting an annual tax rebate to all his state's residents. Since its inception in 1982, the dividend program (Alaska's rebate) has put more than $5 billion directly into Alaskans' pockets.

"Where did Alaska find the money to do this?" you ask. You've probably never heard of anything like it. That's because there's nothing else anywhere in the world quite like the Alaskan dividend.

To pinpoint the Alaskan dividend's genesis, go back nearly thirty years. At that time, Texas, with its rich reserves in the Gulf of Mexico, was the nation's unrivaled oil producer. No other state came close. But all that changed. Huge oil reserves were discovered in Alaska's Prudhoe Bay. The state had literally hit a gold mine of untapped wealth! Impressive as it was, this was not the state's biggest stroke of luck. It was not the state's greatest asset. Instead, the prescience of the state's political leaders was. With the leaders' creativity, the state's gigantic oil reserves turned out to be the catalyst for a much bigger, more permanent innovation that has benefited Alaskans every year for nearly twenty years now. And it will benefit every Alaskan every year forever.

In a rare stroke of genius, the state's political leaders determined that they could transform the benefits from Alaska's finite oil reserves into something permanent. "Who says the income has to stop when the oil runs dry?" they thought. So, they imposed a fee on the oil producers' revenues and placed the resulting proceeds into the Alaska Permanent Fund. The fund's assets were then invested competitively to earn a return, but the principal itself could never be drawn down.

Bureaucrats managing money? This notion is appalling.

Considering their track record, the fund would have been depleted by now!

But the state's political leaders knew what we all know. No bureaucrat could ever be entrusted to manage any money wisely, let alone other people's money. So, instead of permitting the state's bureaucrats to mismanage the money, they created an independent corporation with its own board of trustees to oversee the fund. Every Alaskan is considered a shareholder of the Permanent Fund, making the fund a sort of state-run mutual fund.

Although it is difficult for a growing number of us to remember it, the late 1970s and early 1980s were a time of roaring inflation. For those who experienced the double-digit inflation, it was something they could never forget. Every year, our dollars could buy less. Today, inflation has been tamed. Prices rise less than 2 percent per year. Even so, you can never know if the inflation demon has been slain for all time or is merely hibernating, waiting to strike again.

If inflation reduced the purchasing power of our money, even money in the bank, what guarantee is there that it would not work its same evil magic on the money in the fund? There is none. Knowing this, Alaska's leaders decided to "inflation-proof" the fund so that its assets—in reality, Alaskans' savings account—would not lose value.

I can already hear cries of protest. "That's impossible!"

Indeed it is. But steps can be taken to minimize the corrosive impact of inflation. In Alaska, inflation-proofing works as follows. In a given year, if inflation reduces the value of the fund's assets by $100 million, $100 mil-

lion of the fund's earnings are plowed back into the fund
to offset inflation's bite.

Once the fund has been inflation-proofed, the truly
exciting part of the story begins. Each year, the fund pays
a dividend to the state's 500,000 residents. Currently,
half the fund's earnings is paid out each year as a dividend, and the other half is retained in the fund.
Consequently, the fund's assets continue to increase, its
earnings increase, and its dividend increases.

Last year, more than half a million Alaskans received
a dividend check of $1,296.54 from the Alaska
Permanent Fund. In 1996 they received $1,130.68. In
1995 the amount was $990.30. This is no small change.
Would you like an extra $1,000 a year? We can dream
about it. Alaskans can count on it!

All told, Alaskans have been receiving their annual
dividend for fifteen years in what is, in substance, the
nation's first tax rebate policy.

Still have some doubts? "So what, Alaskans have been
getting a lot of money. The real issue isn't that they have
gotten the money, the real issue is what they have done
with it." Let's ask the Alaskans! In the fall of 1994 the
Alaska Permanent Fund Corporation, the entity charged
with running the fund, mailed a confidential survey to
Alaskans to find out how they had been using their dividend. Let's see what they said.

"Every year I've bought something I needed for my
home, which is fifty-three years old. So far I've bought a
refrigerator, freezer, couch, and swivel rockers, adjustable
bed (I'm disabled), dinette set, oil drum, washer and
dryer, electric range, carpet, clothes, and food," one

explained. "I am sixty-nine years old. This dividend helps me with my winter electric bills, needed service on my old car, and a little something at Christmas for my four grandchildren," another revealed. Another older Alaskan confided, "I am a senior citizen, and I am saving the funds for the time when I will need daily care." These examples are hardly a waste of money.

"We have saved all Permanent Fund dividends for the last ten years to fund our children's education at the University of Alaska. Without the dividend, we would not be able to finance their college education," another said. This is a sound investment for the future of your children.

"Of our three dividends, one will be used to pay off a current student loan, a second will be put toward our son's future education, and the third put toward retirement and daily cost of living," another stated. Few decisions could be more responsible.

One parent, who is undoubtedly still suffering from the hangover of having had to raise teenagers, exclaimed that the dividend offered "[a] chance to be independent of my children." Raising teenagers can be trying.

Another who wished to stay at home with her preschool-age children was equally thankful. "It has allowed me to stay home with my preschoolers instead of going to work."

"I'm four years old. My parents gave me one percent of my dividend (almost $10!) to spend carefully on what I want. [The other f]ifty percent goes to my future education, and 49 percent goes to living expenses and hopefully a family vacation." Thanks to the dividend, this young Alaskan is already learning to make some of life's major decisions.

And in what could be the most compelling arguments for the National Tax Rebate, one observed, "Dividends represent one-sixth of my family's gross income, without which we would have to join the welfare rolls...." Another noted, "During the Alaska economic downturn in the late eighties, the dividends literally kept me afloat. Now that I am working steadily, I endeavor to save the money for the next financial downturn." And still another, "It helps us make an extra house payment every year. It means some savings in the bank to help make ends meet when my husband gets laid off in the winter. (He's a carpenter)." "I live on a very limited income, and each fall it is spent on topping off the fuel tank, tuning the furnace, etc. It greatly lessens the financial burden of winter in Fairbanks." The Alaska dividend buys self-sufficiency. The National Tax Rebate would similarly buy independence and protection from economic downturns.

Of course, not every Alaskan thinks the dividend is the best use of the Permanent Fund's assets. "As state revenues decline and we can no longer maintain our state infrastructure, it will become an embarrassment." But this response is the exception. As with any use of money, there will always be some who think the money could be better spent. And there's no crime in that.

More typical, however, are the following comments. "The Permanent Fund signifies pride to me. The way Alaska manages its savings account is a model to all other states on fiscal management." When was the last time anyone said that about our federal government? "I love the Permanent Fund," another wrote. Finally, someone declared, "I am so very grateful to my state." When was the last time anyone thanked Washington for anything? Better yet, when was the last time Washington deserved to be thanked for anything?

Overall, when asked how they planned to use the current year's dividend, 25 percent said that they planned to save it, 33 percent said they planned to spend it, and 42 percent said that they would save some and spend some. Of those planning to spend at least some of their dividend, 95 percent said that they would spend some or all of it in Alaska. Nearly half said that they would use the dividend to pay off bills and help meet their daily living expenses. Of those planning to save some or all of their dividend, more than 75 percent said that they would save at least half their dividend. Of those saving, 30 percent said that their savings would be used for education, 24 percent to protect against hard times, 20 percent for retirement, and 11 percent for vacation. In short, their plans were scarcely flamboyant. What would you do if you received the Alaska dividend? Think about it for a moment. More than likely your plans would be little different from those of the Alaskans.

All in all, the Permanent Fund Corporation's study found the dividend enormously beneficial to the state's residents. In 1994 alone, the $527 million dividend led to the creation of nearly seven thousand jobs in Alaska, or roughly thirteen jobs for every million dollars. The program has brought more money into the Alaskan economy than the total payroll of every private industry except the oil industry.

The dividend has given Alaskans a huge opportunity to save for such things as college tuition, down payments on homes or cars, or retirement. For example, a family of four that saves its entire dividend from now through 2006 would amass savings of nearly $68,000 just by investing their dividend in thirty-year U.S. Treasury bonds.

Today, the Alaska dividend exceeds $5,000 for each eligible family of four. It has been a boon both for the state's economy and its residents. Imagine what a National Tax Rebate on the order of $12,000 for every American family of four could do.

★ ★ ★

TAX REBATES WORK. People love them. Today, a growing number of states are exploring them.

In February of this year, Governor John Rowland of Connecticut submitted a budget proposal to his state legislature that called for a one-time tax rebate that would refund $125 million of the state's projected $180 million surplus to its taxpayers. In the past, such a surplus would have resulted in a blizzard of new spending proposals. Not any more.

"When I took office…, the people of Connecticut had endured almost a full decade of increasing taxes, deficits, a paralyzing budget crisis and an economy in shambles. But that's all behind us now," the governor explained. "If the people of Connecticut pay more in taxes than we need to finance the cost of government, then they deserve a rebate. It's their money. They earned it…. Let's give it back."

Should the state continue to enjoy budget surpluses, more rebates might be in the offing. Indeed, State Comptroller Nancy Wyman has suggested that the state adopt a program that would provide tax rebates every year the state has a surplus.

Nutty proposals? No. The past practices that allowed state bureaucrats to throw taxpayers' money, the money the taxpayers worked hard to earn and the bureaucrats not at all to take, at their pet projects were the sham. This abuse of taxpayer wallets was a silent scandal that went unnoticed for far too long. But times are changing, even if the bureaucrats are loathe to accept it. Soon, they will have little choice but to yield.

Connecticut is not the first state to propose a tax rebate. "The last time I heard of people getting checks like that [refunding state surpluses through tax rebates] in the mail was in California in the heyday of the booming economy," Arthur Perez, a fiscal analyst with the National Conference of State Legislatures, recounted. In 1987 Governor George Deukmejian of California returned a $1 billion surplus to the state's taxpayers in the form of a tax rebate. In addition, the Alaska dividend—a tax rebate of another kind—has been in place for nearly two decades.

Connecticut's tax rebate proposal is not the first such initiative, nor will it be the last. The tax rebate movement is gaining momentum all around the nation. The concept is not an idea out of left field, it is a mainstream idea. Today, in addition to Connecticut, six other states are looking into tax rebates of various kinds. New York is considering providing Long Islanders a rebate of as much as \$232 on their electric bills. Colorado, Missouri, Oregon, Ohio, and Minnesota are working on tax rebates, as well.

Although the future of Connecticut's planned tax rebate is far from certain this year due to numerous political hurdles, prospects for the movement as a whole are bright. Regardless of the outcome in the Constitution State or the six other states, the evidence in support of tax rebates continues to accumulate. Accordingly, the long-term prospects can only grow brighter.

TO DATE, WITH THE exception of Alaska, states have implemented or introduced tax rebates that refund to taxpayers budget surpluses or other specific tax windfalls. In California, it was a billion-dollar budget surplus. Similarly, in Connecticut, Colorado, Oregon, Ohio, Minnesota, and Missouri, any tax rebates will be refunds of surpluses. In New York, the rebate is a little different. There, the tax rebate would refund part of Long Island's electric ratepayers' electricity expenditures.

If tax rebates are good ways to return budget surpluses or electricity payments, who says their application cannot be made broader? Tax rebates return money. It does not matter whether that money comes from a state sales tax, an income tax, or public utility electric payments. Tax rebates refund money efficiently and effectively.

Why not take the next big step and use tax rebates as a vehicle by which any government—federal, state, or local—could better administer its expenditures?

Government spends taxpayer money to address what it perceives are public needs. Once the high costs of inefficiency and administration are considered, government spending as it currently exists is a most inefficient means for resolving public policy needs. Why not cut out the high costs of government's expensive middleman—the combined costs of administration and waste—and give the money, our money, back to us? Why not give us the resources to solve our own problems? Government's paternalistic approach has failed. We have already seen the consequences of its lost war on poverty, its increasingly confiscatory tax policies. Over and over again, we have lived through its failures. Now is the time for a new approach. To preserve paternalistic government can only be a national travesty. It hasn't solved any problems. And it *can't* solve any problems.

Tax rebates are vastly superior to paternalistic government. They have held up well under rigorous academic scrutiny. They have worked extremely well in practice. Now one last frontier remains for the National Tax Rebate: how it would transform each of our own lives.

CHAPTER 5

Demonstration Tax Rebates

MONOPOLY IS ONE OF the most popular board games ever devised. Its popularity stems less from the fun of playing it than because monopoly is really the "game" of life transposed on a board. Monopoly is about the pursuit of success. It's about taking advantage of your opportunities. It's about making something of yourself. What better satisfaction than that earned in the heat of competition? Everybody plays by the same rules, but you prevail through your own resourcefulness, from the choices you make and do not make. You do it yourself!

But that's not all. Not only does the game have an ideal beginning in which every player starts out equal (all players start with $1,500 in cash) and has real resources to chase his or her destiny, but the game is also about redemption. People make mistakes. We all do. That's life. But Monopoly gives people repeated opportunities to make up for their stumbles, to learn from their errors. Each time a player passes "Go" he or she receives $200. It doesn't matter whether the player has amassed an empire of property replete with houses and hotels or is desperately trying to stave off bankruptcy. Every player is treated alike. Monopoly does not discriminate. Over and over again, it gives people new chances to rise from their falls. To quote the Reverend Jesse Jackson, it "keeps hope alive." Until the end, victory can truly be anybody's. It is this aspect of the game, I believe, that sets Monopoly apart from all others. We all aspire to a world where we can begin on an equal footing, where we can have faith in the future, and where we can create the lives we choose. Monopoly gives us that world.

★ ★ ★

THE WORLD IN WHICH we live and the world of Monopoly are two starkly different places. We don't all begin on an equal footing. Perfect equality is never possible. But we can make the two far more alike. A universal National Tax Rebate would do just that. Every person would have seed money with which to begin his or her journey. Each person would have the freedom to try new things, take some chances—in short, build the life he or she truly desires.

There is strong evidence from the state level and academic research that a rebate would be both economically and politically viable. But all this falls short, because it tells us nothing about what a rebate might mean to America's families. Nor does it say what a rebate would mean to each one of us.

The Institute for SocioEconomic Studies set out to explore this question and study first-hand the effects of such a program by awarding demonstration rebates of $1,000 a month for twenty years to three American families. In order to identify the three families, we needed to get in touch with Americans all across the nation. So, in early 1997, ISES took out ads in numerous newspapers and on radio shows across the country, including *USA Today*, asking people to respond to the following questions: Tell us what you'd do with an extra $1,000 a month; and would you trade government benefits for a monthly check? To encourage individuals and families to respond, the institute broadcast that it would select three families from all those who wrote back, and award them a demonstration tax rebate of $1,000 a month for twenty years. Every American household with a dependent child and not receiving Social Security or SSI benefits would be eligible for one of the awards. We asked interested families to write ISES a two-page letter telling us how an extra $1,000 a month would improve their lives and help them build a brighter future. Applicants were informed that their essays would be judged on what was written, not how well it was written. In addition, for research purposes we asked that the letters include whether the respondents considered themselves high-income, middle-income, or low-income earners; whether anyone in the household was employed; and whether any household member was currently receiving government assistance. Not coincidentally, the deadline for submissions was April 15, 1997. What better reminder could there be than your own tax return that Americans need tax relief?

The response was overwhelming. Families from all fifty states—from New York to Hawaii—responded. Stacks of letters—from working class families, mothers on welfare, even one budding poet—arrived daily.

"This letter is in response to your appearance on the UBN Radio Network and the $1,000 a month for 20 years offer. In order to qualify for this offer, I will answer your questions as they pertain to us.

"Our family consists of the following members: David, age 3, Katie, age 7, Billy, age 11, and my wife, Shelley (37) and myself (44). We are not receiving any government assistance and hope we never need it. The most money we have ever earned before taxes is about $28,000/year. We are currently starting a small business.

"So far as our family is concerned, the reason a tax rebate is preferable to the current 'social engineering' tax code, is illustrated by the following examples:

1. We have paid thousands a year in medical insurance but not enough to itemize.
2. We have earned too little to be comfortable but too much to qualify for the 'Earned Income Credit.'
3. We have paid punitive amounts of tax when self-employed.
4. Combination of 3 & 4—i.e., Earn optimum amount to qualify for maximum EITC (poverty level) and give it back to pay self-employment tax.

"The reason it is better for the families to decide what to spend the tax relief on is because the government cannot possibly anticipate family needs that constantly change. For instance, this month the car might need repairs. Next month, school supplies, medical expenses, or clothing could be the issue. Further, the government has no right to presume that they should micro-manage our lives via the tax code.

"As to what effect an award of $1,000 a month for 20 years would have on our family's lifestyle, I would have to say it would be profound. It would provide a feeling of security and relief to know that the essential bills and expenses would be that much easier to afford during periods of low income. During 'normal' periods, it would reduce the number of times we are forced to choose between 'semi-essential' items (new shoes for one child vs. new glasses for another).

"Thank you for your consideration."

William P.
Arizona

★ ★ ★

"MY NAME IS CHANDRA W. I am 26 years old and am the single parent of a seven-year-old-son and three-year-old twin daughters. Like many single parents, I am on welfare. My experiences on welfare include the embarrassment of using food stamps and a Medicaid card, dealing with landlords who think because I am on welfare I have no pride in my home or surroundings, and I am made to feel ashamed because I can't pay for things with my own hard-earned money. I am in college, currently in my third trimester. In one more year I will have an AVS Degree in Paralegal Studies. Welfare asked me to drop out of school to take a workfare assignment. When I refused, they took away my car fare and child care money. In spite of this, I continue to go to school. I rely on family to baby-sit and stretch my welfare check to the limit so that I can have car fare to go back and forth to school. I want to get a part-time job, but welfare will cut me off completely and I wouldn't be able to take care of my children, pay bills, and go to school.

"If I had $1,000 a month I would use it to help with my education and get off welfare. I would say good-bye to welfare and get a part-time job. My children would have money put aside each month for college. Not only would it change my life and give me a sense of pride, it would ensure that my children would have a chance at the lives they deserve. With each passing semester, my head lifts a little. I look forward to the day it can be raised forever. I know that I can do it and I will."

Chandra W.
New York

★ ★ ★

"WHAT WOULD I DO with an extra twelve grand?

"For that thousand a month, here's what I've got planned:

Bonjour to filets, *adios* corned beef hash—

The sky is the limit with third-party cash.

Eating out more than monthly would be really nice,

Especially to order ignoring the price.

But the very first thing, once the check clears the banks,

is to call Leonard Greene and give him my thanks—

Maybe send him some Cubans, a magnum of Dom,
Invite him for dinner, and a date with my Mom.

Things would be different with twelve grand for years:
I'd be in the black, instead of arrears.
I'd pay off the balance on each credit card—
Visa, Discovery, and Montgomery Ward.
I'd pay off the note on my Chevy "Classique"
And buy me a car that's not an antique.
I'd undo the default at my old *alma mater*
And attend our homecoming a *persona* who's *grata*
Of what would be left—a handsome amount—
I'd put every cent in a savings account!

Well, not *every* cent—there's so much to do
With twelve grand a year, for twenty years too!
I might make provision, in case of disaster,
To ensure that yours truly remains his own master.
I might purchase a policy, term or whole life,
Benefiting my children and my home schooling wife.
I might line up a health plan that covers things dental
(Even more comprehensive in case I go mental).
I could afford these things now, were it not for my
tax—
I'm one of those wretches who've fallen through
cracks.

Twelve grand is the total (nearly exact)
Amount of my earnings Uncle Sam will extract.
That's quite a large portion, but what's got me burned:
I'll never see twelve grand in service returned.
Domestic tranquillity and the common defense
Are the only two items that are worth the expense.

And who can depend, in his golden old days,
On the pittance that Social Security pays?
We all know the System is not even sound;
By the time we retire, it won't be around.

Twelve grand's the down payment on the decent-sized house
I'd love to provide for my children and spouse.
If we just had the money, if only we could,
We'd much rather live in a nice neighborhood.
A backyard with a fence and a swing set would keep
Our kids out of mischief—and out of the street.
We'd have room to spread out, we could really relax
With money left over after paying our tax.
We're cramped in this rental: four kids and one bath.
"Accidents" waiting to happen; it's just basic math.

There are other investments I'd make with twelve grand—
If my after-tax income exceeded demand.
I'd buy stocks and bonds with my yearly rebates,
Rare books, stamps and coins, and collectible plates.
I'd invest in myself, maybe learn a new skill,
Some trade to fall back on when I'm over the hill.
I'd invest in my children, to help them excel,
And then, in my dotage, they might treat me well.
Yet another investment that pays dividends
Is to spend some time traveling and making new friends.

With twelve grand a year, I'd no longer be penniless.
For once in my life, I could afford to be generous.
I could give to the church a sizable sum

Or set up an annual scholarship fund.
I could sponsor a mission and some needy kid.
I could sponsor a contest, just like you did.
I could hire some musicians to play in the park
Or pay pyrotechnicians to light up the dark.
I'd want to do *something* to share my good luck
And let everyone know I'm not tight with a buck.

There, now I've told you all that I've planned
For what I would do with an extra twelve grand.
If my entry is chosen, I'll be really glad,
but I have to admit that I'll also be mad.
I'll be glad to be given such a wonderful gift,
But the gift will remind me of why I'm so miffed:
Uncle Sam takes too much of the money I've earned.
He must have forgotten what the British Crown
learned.
Say, twelve grand is just enough to launch a crusade
To remind our great country of the promise
betrayed!"

F. R. D.
Missouri

★ ★ ★

"I RECENTLY READ A newspaper article concerning
your prototype 'tax rebate' plan. This is one of the most
sensible proposals that I have heard in a long time. I agree
that the country would best be served by placing more
money in the hands of its citizens and less in the hands
of the sprawling federal bureaucracy which is so far
removed from the individual needs of the citizens. I
believe that the vast majority of U.S. citizens are respon-

sible human beings who can best manage their own financial resources if they are allowed to by the government. I would like to make my case for being chosen as one of your $1,000 per month trial rebate recipients. I believe that my family is typical of many in today's middle class.

"First, let me give you a description of my family. My wife and I have been married for 18 years. I am 40 years of age and she is 38. We are both teachers. She teaches 2nd grade at the local elementary school (12 years' experience) and I teach math at a community college in a nearby town (18 years' experience). We have three young children, ages 7, 9 and 10. We have a house (with a $75,000 mortgage) and two cars. My wife and I both have parents who are still living. Neither of us expects to inherit a large amount of money from our families.

"Before I explain how $1,000 a month for 20 years would change the way I live, let me first explain how we now live. We are not poor or starving. We have a house to live in and manage to keep food on the table. We manage to buy clothes and shoes for ourselves and our children. We are usually able to keep the bills paid each month, except perhaps around Christmas time. We try to take a short vacation each summer. In other words, we are not destitute or even needy.

"But like many American families in our income range (about $65,000 annual income for the family), we feel the pinch of the large amount of our salaries which is taken each month by the federal government. Some months it is a struggle to make ends meet. We try to budget our income each month. We are not extravagant or wasteful. For example, my wife and I both drive vehicles with more than 100,000 miles on them. So although we do manage to live each month, we are not able to improve our financial situation due to the constant drain on our resources by federal, state, and local taxes.

"Recent studies have shown that the American people are saving less money than ever before. I believe that the main reason for this is a larger portion of our money is going to support the federal bureaucracy. Lower- and middle-income families simply require all of their paycheck to maintain a decent standard of living. Therefore, savings are usually the first item to disappear from the family budget.

"How would $1,000 per month change the way we live? One important area where this would help us would be in savings. In our current financial condition, we simply are not able to save sufficiently each month. There are always unexpected "emergencies" which seem to quickly drain the small amount we do put in savings. As a result, we sometimes rely on credit cards when we really should not. This puts the additional strain of extra interest to pay on our budget. A portion of the $1,000 would be used to establish a 'safety net' savings account equal to about one month's pay. This extra savings cushion would greatly improve our budgeting process.

"Most families in our income level also find it difficult to save for long-term expenses such as college. While we do have some money set aside for college, it will not be enough to meet the expected expenses, even at state-supported four-year colleges. With three children it would simply require more than our current budget allows to completely prepare for these estimated expenses. This means that either we will have to borrow money to pay for our children's education or they will have to take out student loans. Therefore, it will be an added burden either to our financial situation or to that of our children. An extra $1,000 per month would allow us to considerably increase the amount we put into our children's college funds. Middle-class children are quickly being squeezed out of the market for attending private universities such as Harvard or Yale. Most middle-class parents simply cannot afford to send their children to such schools, even if the student has the ability and desire to attend.

"Another important area where an extra $1,000 per month would improve our way of life would be in the quality of life. I am not referring to being able to buy more expensive products, but to being able to spend more quality time with our families. Many middle-income families find it necessary to work longer hours or take a second job just to make ends meet. I, for example, teach night classes one or two nights per week for extra income to make ends meet. If it were not for this extra income, we would have to do without some quality enhancing extras such as our family vacation. The percentage of people working two jobs is higher now than it has ever been in the history of our country. This is due in large part to wage erosion by government taxes. This not only causes the person to be away from the family for more hours, but also produces stress and fatigue which reduces the quality of the time that they do manage to spend with the family. An extra $1,000 per month would allow these people to forego the second job. This would also have the added benefit of opening up the job market for the unemployed.

"These are just a few of the benefits that could be recognized from having an extra $1,000 per month in the budget of each American family. To reiterate, I believe that the American people should be able to judge for themselves how to allocate their financial resources. I believe they would do a much better job than the government. Please consider this as my application to be one of the rebate recipients in your study."

Larry N.
Mississippi

★ ★ ★

AFTER BEING SORTED and read, each letter was entered into a database. Two clear observations could be made: one, American families responded overwhelmingly in support of the National Tax Rebate, and two, the letters showcased that American families would put the rebate money to good use. Of the responses, 67 percent said they would invest in their children's education or their own education, 59 percent said the Rebate would allow one parent to stay at home with their young children, 38 percent would improve their housing, and 25 percent would purchase health insurance for their family. Our letters were Alaska revisited.

THIS IS A SNAPSHOT OF WHAT AMERICANS SAID IN THEIR LETTERS:

"When I read the article [about the National Tax

Rebate], I had no choice but to respond," wrote a woman from Greensboro, North Carolina. "I am responding because I feel as if someone—YOU—has tapped into reality as far as helping the American people."

"Writing this letter has helped me to start dreaming again," commented a single mother of three from Tennessee. "I want to show my kids that work pays better than welfare," said another woman from Florida. "Right now it doesn't." And a family from Missouri that defines itself as "middle class" summed it up by writing, "We don't dream big anymore... thank you for getting us dreaming again."

We're learning that mainstream America doesn't want a safety net, but a safety ladder. Letters from all across America repeat the same theme. People want to improve their lives and know better than the government what they need to get the job done.

A mother from Oklahoma discussed the possibility of getting off welfare with a rebate and foresaw that, "instead of bringing up another generation of hopelessness, it [the rebate] will help bring a new generation of hopefulness."

"$1,000 a month in lieu of a myriad of government programs," writes an AFDC mother, "would make my family a part of the American Dream—not just a bystander."

A family in Illinois sums it up by writing that a National Tax Rebate would "encourage people to be better workers, to rely more on themselves and build pride within them. Everyone wants a better chance to get ahead in life. That was what our country was founded on." They believe a National Tax Rebate would "continue to keep the dreams of millions of Americans alive and prospering." Their letter ends: "Keep this wonderful country what it always has been—a country where dreams come true!"

★ ★ ★

ALTHOUGH THE INSTITUTE was able to offer demonstration tax rebates to only three families, I believe that every family deserves the National Tax Rebate.

In the letters we received, people from all across the country shared with us their frustration with the present situation, and their intense desire for real middle-class tax relief. The National Tax Rebate would provide this and an opportunity for every person who is in financial difficulties to experience the American Dream. One Midwest mother of two wrote us that "the American Dream is dying for many." Perhaps the Dream is not yet dead—I know it isn't—but for many it is still just a dream.

Despite working hard, getting an education, and playing by the rules, we learned that a lot of Americans feel cheated. And why shouldn't they? Today, many middle-class families describe their economic circumstances as handicapped, even if the government doesn't. "I think that people who are not at the poverty level but who do not earn enough money to feel a sense of security go unnoticed in society," is what another woman wrote. A clever homemaker described her family and millions of other middle-class Americans as "financially challenged."

Americans want to regain control of their lives today because they're finding that many of the institutions to which we've relinquished control are out of touch with our needs and seem more intent on serving their own needs.

Contrary to the belief of Washington's bureaucrats, if Americans were given control over the spending of their tax dollars, the money would be spent wisely. No, the money would not be used to buy a shiny new sports car or a trip to Vegas. You would not blow the cash on conspicuous consumption, frivolous luxuries, and decadent indulgences. The letters we received suggested that the dreams Americans have pertaining to the rebate are modest and intensely practical, but varied (no different from those of the Alaskans). That's part of the beauty of the rebate. The rebate program would allow individuals to choose how to spend their own money, based on their own unique priorities, not the government's.

Give a man a fish, goes the old truism, and you feed the man for a day. Teach the man to fish, and you feed him for a lifetime. Americans still understand this today and, if given a tax rebate, most Americans would buy one fish and spend the rest of the money on a fishing pole, bait, and angling lessons.

A rebate not only holds promise for tax relief, it also provides, potentially, the means to tear down the many economic obstacles to financial independence that the existing welfare state has erected and preserved. A transparent, self-directed approach to welfare based on trust and compassion is essential to truly ending welfare as we know it. The National Tax Rebate is founded on trust in the individual and compassion for those in need.

The rebate assumes that government should not do

for you what you can and should do for yourself. It is built on the premise that no one can do a better job of looking out for you and your family than you can. Simple, proven, and universally understood ideas, except by those living within the Washington Beltway's fantasyland.

Press Conference on Capitol Hill

A press conference was held in Washington, DC, on July 23, 1997, to introduce the three families who were awarded the demonstration tax rebates and to present additional information on how a tax rebate would work. The press conference was the first in a series of coordinated steps for building national awareness of the tax rebate concept. The conference received national coverage by the print media and was featured in numerous television and radio news spots. At the same press conference, the institute released a study of five conceptual tax rebate plans based on an analysis prepared for the institute by Columbia University Professor Irwin Garfinkel. Using data from the March 1995 Current Population Survey of the U.S. Census Bureau, the study examines the impact of a tax rebate on poverty in the United States.

In my remarks, I made the point that while the National Tax Rebate is aimed squarely at achieving tax relief for the middle class, many other benefits would follow. The virtual eradication of poverty, new job creation, improved balance of trade, decreased bureaucracy, improved conditions in our inner cities—a National Tax Rebate would accomplish all this and much more.

NATIONAL TAX REBATE
DEMONSTRATION FAMILIES

Three families—the Coverts, the Hammonds, and the Butlers—were awarded demonstration tax rebates at this press conference in Washington, DC. These families were selected from the thousands of families who responded to our national media campaign. Each is now receiving a demonstration rebate of $1,000 a month for the next twenty years, funded by ISES, as the Institute's ongoing research into the feasibility of the National Tax Rebate. ISES hopes that the impact of these sample rebates will illustrate to all Americans the potential benefits of a national rebate. While each of the families' individual situations differ, they represent all Americans in their desire to improve the quality of their lives.

The Coverts

Rural Illinois is home to Allan and Teresa Covert, where they live on the family farm with their teenage chil-

The Covert Family

THE NATIONAL TAX REBATE

dren, Cassandra and Christopher. As on many farms, the entire family shares in the work. They farm about 1,800 acres of row crops, maintain a herd of about 150 cows, and raise 800 to 1,000 cattle a year in a confinement unit. In response to the survey questions, Teresa wrote, "We have struggled through the hard times of 18 percent interest, droughts, and two flood years… barely managing to hang on to our farm operation." She wrote of their hopes to send their two children to college. Unfortunately, this would place them in a double bind. The expenses of college would have to be added to the cost of hiring extra help on the farm to handle the chores currently performed by their children. Since being awarded their demonstration rebate, the Coverts have paid off their car loan and paid down some of their farm loans. Thanks to their sample rebate, they look to the future with more confidence than ever. They now expect that the family farm will remain a part of the Covert family for generations to come.

The Hammond Family

The Hammonds

"The Hammond family is definitely the kind of family that [the] Institute is seeking to investigate the viability of a national tax rebate plan. We are the working poor who are grasping for middle class," wrote Darlene Hammond of Colorado. Her husband, Arthur, has worked as a machinist for almost twenty years, rising through the ranks to his present position of shop supervisor. At one time, when Arthur was working at minimum wage, the family briefly resorted to food stamps to help provide for the needs of their three young children. But, when Arthur and Darlene were told that they would have to put their children in a day care center to continue to receive assistance, they refused. Even if it meant losing their food stamps, and it did, there was no way that they were going to let Washington's bureaucrats tell them how to raise their children. This was certainly not an easy decision as it placed additional hardship on the struggling family, but that's how important it was, and still is, to Arthur and Darlene to care for their children themselves.

At the time the Hammonds were awarded their demonstration rebate, they had lived for many years in a mobile home where, in addition to Arthur's job and the two boys' after-school jobs, Arthur and Darlene worked as onsite managers of the mobile-home park. They had never lived in a house of their own. The rebate has helped them finance the purchase of their first home. Now that they have completed their move, they will no longer have to endure being called "trailer trash." In addition to using their rebate to help make their home mortgage payments, the Hammonds are also setting aside part of their rebate to provide for their children's education.

The Butlers

Hurricane Andrew was the most destructive storm ever to hit the United States. The Butler family was one of the thousands of families in Florida and Louisiana to be devastated by Andrew's wrath. When Hurricane Andrew came ashore, it destroyed Ivy Butler's auto detailing business, and forced him, his wife Donna, and their two daughters to move in with Donna's parents in a suburb of Baton Rouge, Louisiana. Starting over, Ivy trained for and obtained a job as a long-distance truck driver. The pay was not bad, but the schedule kept him away

The Butler Family

from home for at least three weeks out of every month, often more. As a result, he missed birthdays, school plays, and daily life with his family. As Donna wrote to the institute, "a $1,000 a month rebate would allow me to keep my family together."

And it is already

beginning to happen. With the help from their tax rebate, Ivy has been able to quit long-distance trucking in favor of less lucrative, but more rewarding, short-haul driving that brings him home each night. There, he is able to help his children with their homework and mow the grass. He again has a family.

The Butlers are currently renting a small house near Donna's parents as Ivy and Donna scout locations where he might reopen his auto detailing business. Over the coming couple of years, the Butlers hope to restart the business and phase it into a full-time operation. Meanwhile, making regular deposits to college savings accounts for their daughters is a high priority.

All these awards are about choice. The three families and the decisions they are making every day are living proof. Each family knows best how to improve its own unique situation. Government programs don't work. They can't. Direct rebates do. It's time for a paradigm shift away from big government to individual choice. I hope that these awards will be the catalyst for a larger national debate.

The institute plans to continue to follow the progress of the three families over the entire twenty-year period they receive their demonstration tax rebates. We look forward to the results and are confident that they will validate what we already expect. People can and do make good decisions.

Demonstration College Rebates

The responses to ISES's national letter campaign provided the basis for both the demonstration tax rebates and demonstration education rebates. The first demonstration Education Rebates were awarded in the fall of 1997. Six students at a local two-year community college, Westchester Community College (WCC), were each given an Education Rebate in the amount of $500 a month, payable only during the students' second year of college. To qualify for the rebate, the applicants were required to demonstrate that they were single parents with one or more children and that they had successfully completed their first year of study. In addition, each applicant was asked to write a letter describing his or her goals and how $500 a month would enable him or her to achieve those goals. As with the National Tax Rebate concept, the responses to the idea were overwhelmingly positive.

Nerrica, a student in the Practical Nursing program wrote, "This money will definitely come in handy for my books and especially for my son's day-care, which is eighty dollars each week." Although Nerrica works per diem at a nursing home, the union she belongs to will pay for only twelve credits or less. Also, the nursing home will reimburse her tuition only at the end of her course. The Education Rebate, along with Nerrica's part-time job, will allow her to pay for and complete her Practical Nursing degree. "Most of my friends gave me the idea that I am trying to do too much at a time," Nerrica confides, "but why should I put something off for next year when I can do it this year—the earlier the better. I believe that where there is a will there is a way, and if I am chosen for this [rebate], I am sure that my path to success will be looking much brighter."

Another college student, and the mother of a three-year-old, said that "Being a single parent and coming off of welfare has been a real struggle for me and the only way that I could do that is to go back to school." A paralegal student, Denise found that Social Services would not approve her request to go to school because she had a secretarial job. "My future goals," Denise reports, "differed from the Department of Social Services because I wanted to have a career/profession, not just a job. Working, going to school full-time, and being a single parent have not always been manageable for me. Sometimes, I worry how I am going to make it both financially and mentally. Also, I worry about being a good mother. It takes money to do a lot of things, and most of the time I don't have the funds to even take her out to McDonald's for a meal. It hurts." After getting off welfare, Denise found a part-time job that, in addition to the rebate, will help defray the costs of college and baby-sitting.

Many of the students who applied for the Education Rebate wrote of seeking to break the cycle of poverty through educational achievement. Vera, one such student, typified the single mother who often finds herself destined to spend a lifetime on public assistance. She is unemployed, lives on Supplemental Security Income (SSI), is a beneficiary of Section 8 housing, and receives food stamps. Prior to moving into subsidized housing, Vera and her one-year-old son lived in a homeless shelter. She decided that she would do something to improve her situation and to break the cycle of poverty, so she enrolled in courses at WCC. We met Vera after she had completed her first year of college. She plans to graduate with a degree in computer science. "Over the past year, my life has undergone many changes toward a brighter future," she writes. "I love school, and feel committed to my education so that I can eventually be completely financially independent and care for my son in the best way possible." Vera wrote that the rebate would help her "pay for child care... while I attend classes and for additional study time. It would help pay for books that are not covered by my TAP award... and toward transportation to and from school. Finally, this money could reduce my fears about my finances so that I could put full attention to my studies." As an Education Rebate recipient, Vera's future looks brighter and so does her son's. For them the cycle of poverty almost certainly will be broken.

CHAPTER 6

Freedom to Succeed

GOVERNMENT AFFECTS EVERY aspect of our lives. From the food we eat, the schools we attend, the doctors we visit, the cars we drive, and the clothing we wear, government is all around us. Whether at home or in the workplace, there is no escaping the long reach of our big, paternalistic government. We are becoming a society in which far-away government bureaucrats make an increasing number of our choices for us. Every day, we lose a little more of our precious freedom. Every day, our ability to create our own futures is diminished.

Today, the federal government has nearly 70,000 pages in regulations, along with an army of 130,000 bureaucrats who create and enforce these regulations. By directing the talents and abilities of these 130,000 people to nonproductive bureaucracy, the government is wasting human resources that could be far better utilized in the productive economy. Today, the federal government also spends $12.5 billion solely on regulatory activities. But this is just a small part of the picture. Government red tape steals nearly $230 billion each year from our productive economy. Price and entry controls stifle the marketplace—our nation's engine of wealth creation—at an additional cost of $220 billion a year. Big government means less freedom, less opportunity, and less wealth for all Americans.

Today, the bureaucrats take and spend an increasing portion of our hard-earned wages for follies that have little to do with our needs. They spend it in the name of the public good. What about our good? That seems irrelevant. What the bureaucrats want is what matters. What we want does not. After all, the bureaucrats have freedom to waste our money any way they want, knowing they have little or no financial stake in the consequences of their actions. So they figure, "Who cares?"

Well, we care. It is *our* money.

Not only has government forgotten whose money it is that it wastes, today's paternalistic government has also forgotten that it obtains its financial sustenance from our productive economy. The private economy is the goose that has been laying the golden eggs that made the United States the strongest wealth-producing machine in the world. Government is sacrificing that wonderful animal by regulating against the mechanisms that produce the golden eggs. It is throwing sand in the whirling gear with regulations and penalties. The goose consists of people willing to take risks, often substantial ones, to create a better life. Government is strangling those risktakers in impenetrable red tape and mindless bureaucracy.

Nevertheless, we still see that daring in the people around us. We might be carrying the heavy burden of big government on our shoulders, but we haven't yet forgotten what it's like to be free. We still yearn for freedom.

I know what a society with less government would be like. I vividly remember life before the rise of our welfare state. Today, government is one of our nation's leading growth industries. For the past sixty years, it has been crowding out some of our best hopes and opportunities. I believe the National Tax Rebate would change all this, and its benefits would be enormous.

The National Tax Rebate, by restoring and increasing individual choice, would result in significant economic gains. There would be an immediate and substantial gain in efficiency that would result from eliminating government waste and inefficiency; estimates of this gain vary from 10 percent to 25 percent of every dollar that is currently being spent, or more accurately, misspent by government. Had the National Tax Rebate been in place for the past ten years, our economy would have generated an additional $1 trillion or more in production. Aside from the Rebate itself, each American would have benefited from a productivity dividend of more than $3,000.

The National Tax Rebate would do more than just increase production. It would further strengthen what is already the world's most competitive and dynamic economy. Much of our economic vitality can be traced to America's entrepreneurs who bring their vivid imaginations to life.

Unlike the multitude of government regulations that impede entrepreneurship, a National Tax Rebate would increase it. First, it would starve many of the bureaucracies, which stifle our entrepreneurs, of the cash they need to survive. More than that, it would provide all Americans with funds that they could use to start their own enterprises. According to the results of a study on business formation by the National Bureau of Economic Research, a National Tax Rebate could increase the probability of one's starting his or her own business by 10 percent to 40 percent.* This is powerful. If our entrepreneurs have made our economy as strong as it currently is, think of how much more formidable it would be with a 10 percent to 40 percent increase in entrepreneurship.

A National Tax Rebate would improve all of our lives. People would be rewarded for working hard. Farmers, large and small alike, would no longer be forced to plow their crops under just to please government bureaucrats. Parents would have the financial ability to send their children to good schools. Low-income families would be liberated from public housing's slums.

Over the past sixty years, Washington's bureaucrats may have forgotten what made America great, but we remember. As Ronald Reagan advised, "Trust the people; believe every human being is capable of greatness, capable of self-government... only when people are free to worship, create, and build, only when they are given a personal stake in deciding their destiny and benefiting from their own risks, only then do societies become dynamic, prosperous, progressive, and free."

From the survey letters the Institute for SocioEconomic Studies received in support of the Rebate, to the responses of Alaska's dividend recipients, people want to control their own lives. They want to chase their best opportunities and dreams. They want to know that they truly do have hope for a better future.

---

*National Bureau of Economic Research, working paper #3252.

The National Tax Rebate would create this kind of America. Every person would again be free to choose opportunity. Every person would again be free to succeed. America would again be the land of promise our Founders envisioned more than two hundred years ago. The America with a National Tax Rebate would truly be a better America with less government.

APPENDIX

The National Tax Rebate Microsimulations of Five Variations

Commissioned by
The Institute for SocioEconomic Studies
July 1997

Conducted by
Prof. Irwin Garfinkel and Chien-Chung Huang
The Columbia University School of Social Work

Coordinated by
Martin R. Cantor, CPA, Senior Fellow
The Institute for SocioEconomic Studies

THE TAX REBATE PLANS

This study examines five hypothetical Tax Rebate Plans. These plans were selected for examination without preference or prejudice to test a range of possibilities.

Benefit Structure

Each of the five tax rebate alternatives examined in this simulation was designed to place a high percentage of families above the poverty threshold, whether the family includes a working adult or not. Poor families with a member who can work could escape from poverty by supplementing the income from a low-paying job with the tax rebate benefits.

The first plan, which we call the Standard Plan, establishes a baseline from which the other plans depart. Under the Standard Plan, all children up to age eighteen would receive a rebate of $2,175 per year, and all adults between the ages of eighteen and sixty-five would receive a $4,000 per year tax rebate. The elderly would receive an $8,000 rebate, or their Social Security payment. The benefit structures of the Standard Plan and the others described below are summarized in Table I.

The Tax Rebate, in all plans, is taxable. The after-tax value of the rebate for people with higher incomes is smaller than for people who have lower incomes. For example, if a person pays a federal income tax rate of 40 percent, the federal after-tax value of a tax rebate of $4,000 is $2,400, while a person trying to escape poverty would be in a position to keep the entire $4,000.

The Children Plus, Adult Plus, and Single Parent Plus plans, respectively, focus higher benefits on children, prime age adults, and single parents. Note from Table I that the Children Plus Plan not only raises the benefits per child from $2,175 to $4,000, but also lowers the benefit per adult from $4,000 to $3,150. Similarly, the Single Parent Plus Plan not only raises the benefit to a single parent from $4,000 to $6,000, but also raises the benefit to all children from $2,175 to $2,700 and lowers the benefit for all other adults to $3,000.

The last plan is a variation of the Adult Plus Plan in

which the beneficiaries of Old Age, Survivors, and Disability Insurance (OASDI) do not participate in the tax rebate plan and would be exempt from cuts in benefits they receive from the federal government.

TABLE 1
The Tax Rebate Plans

Plan Name	Annual Benefits	Financing
Standard Plan	Elderly (E) $8,000; Adult (A) $4,000; Children (C) $2,175 OASDI kept harmless.	Offsets from OASDI. Elimination of 115 programs. Elimination of personal exemptions. Taxation of tax rebate.
Children Plus Plan	E $8,000; A $3,150; C $4,000 OASDI kept harmless.	Offsets from OASDI. Elimination of 115 programs. Elimination of personal exemptions. Taxation of tax rebate.
Single Parent Plus Plan	E $8,000; First A with children $6,000; Other A $3,000; C $2,700 OASDI kept harmless.	Offsets from OASDI. Elimination of 115 programs. Elimination of personal exemptions. Taxation of tax rebate.
Adult Plus Plan	E $8,000; A $6,000; C $2,000 OASDI kept harmless.	Offsets from OASDI. Elimination of 115 programs. Elimination of personal exemptions. Taxation of tax rebate. Inclusion of state funding participation.
Social Security Out Plan	A $6,000; C $2,000 The beneficiaries of OASDI and SSI are left out of tax rebate plan.	Elimination of 113 programs. Elimination of personal exemptions. Taxation of tax rebate. Inclusion of state funding participation.

Financing of the Tax Rebate Plans

In four of the five rebate plans, the tax rebates are financed solely by the revenue raised from eliminating personal exemptions and taxing the rebates, by offsets from OASDI, and by the elimination of 115 federal programs. Table 2 illustrates how the Standard Plan would be financed. In 1994, there were approximately 70 million children, 160 million non-aged adults, and 30 million aged adults. Thus, the gross costs of the Standard Plan total $1.031 trillion. Making the tax rebate taxable and eliminating exemptions raises an additional $288 billion, reducing the net cost of the tax rebate to $743 billion.

TABLE 2
Financing the Tax Rebate Plan (Millions $)

Program	1994 Budget
I. Gross Costs of Tax Rebates	1,030,888
II. Financing	1,031,418
1. Revenue from Taxing Tax Rebate	169,851
2. Eliminating Personal Exemptions	118,227
3. Offsets in Social Security: The amounts of Old Age, Survivors, and Disability Insurance ($312.84 billion) minus harmlessness costs of Standard Plan ($37.15 billion)	275,694
4. Elimination of Federal Programs	467,646
A. Tax Exemption/Exclusions	256,400
B. Direct Income Support Programs	89,845
C. Special Needs/Social Services	48,057
D. Housing	36,406
E. Business/Economic Development	14,883
F. Student Loans	9,033
G. Farm Subsidies/Price Supports	8,616
H. Employment Programs	4,406

As described above, recipients of OASDI would receive either their existing OASDI benefits or the tax rebate, whichever is higher. In 1994, OASDI beneficiaries received $313 billion. Since they would receive either the tax rebate or their OASDI benefit, but not both, most of the cost of the tax rebate for these beneficiaries would be offset by existing OASDI benefits. Indeed, as Table 2 shows, all but $37 billion of the current cost of OASDI, or $276 billion, would offset the cost of the tax rebate.

The last section of Table 2 contains a list of the programs that would be replaced by the tax rebate. The budget numbers included in this part of the table are the latest information available at the time this microsimulation was conducted; they can be found in one or the other of two government-published records that reflect actual expenses: *The 1993 Green Book* or *The 1995 Catalog of Federal Domestic Assistance*. As indicated in Table 2, total expenditures for the excluded programs were $467 billion in 1994. This amount included $256 billion of Tax Exemptions/Exclusions, $90 billion of Direct Income Support Programs, $48 billion of Special Needs and Social Service Programs, $36 billion of Housing Subsidies, $15 billion of Business and Economic Development, $9 billion of Student Loans, $9 billion of Farm Subsidies and Price Supports, and $4 billion of Employment Programs.

The projected Adult Plus Plan requires additional financing. A substantial portion of this additional financing could come from recapture of the state tax windfall that would result from the increase in state taxable income due to the taxability of the Tax Rebate.

RESULTS

The results of the five microsimulations are illustrated in Tables 3, 4, and 5. Table 3 highlights the changes in the poverty rate from the pretransfer, pretax to the current system and to each of the five tax rebate plans. It also shows the aggregate poverty gap of the current system and the rebate alternatives. Table 4 presents information on the effectiveness of each plan in the vertical distribution of income. The population is divided into fifths or quintiles from the bottom to the top, or from the poorest to the richest families. Table 5 also presents information on the effects of the tax rebates on the horizontal distribution of income by indicating the percent of "winners" and "losers," as well as the mean increase and decrease in earnings within each quintile of the population. A winner is a family for which the income will increase more than 10 percent; a loser is a family for which the income will decrease more than 10 percent. It is our assumption that a change in income of 10 percent or more is a significant change for any family.

The Effect on Poverty

All five tax rebate plans reduced the aggregate poverty rate and the aggregate poverty gap. This is true no matter which assumption is made about the value of in-kind benefits to recipients. In a few cases, some subgroups were made worse off, if we assume that the worth of in-kind benefits to recipients is 100 percent of its cost to taxpayers. This assumption is clearly false. Recipients gain nothing from administrative costs. We confine the rest of the comparisons to the assumption that recipients value the benefits at only 75 percent of cost. We believe that to be the most scientifically accurate assumption.

The Adult Plus Plan did the best job of reducing the poverty rate—from 10 percent to under 6 percent when there were no labor supply improvements, and to under 2 percent with labor supply improvements. These would be significant improvements. Similarly, the poverty gap would be cut by more than half even without a change in labor supply—from $42 billion to $17 billion, and with a large labor supply response, to less than $10 billion.

The Child Plus Plan, which requires the same financing as the Standard Plan, did almost as good a job as the Adult Plus Plan in reducing the poverty rate and poverty gap. The Child Plus Plan also did a better job of reducing child poverty, reducing it to 8 percent as compared to 11 percent for the Adult Plus Plan.

With the exception of the Social Security Out Plan, all plans provide the elderly with an $8,000 benefit. This rebate would immediately raise virtually all elderly recipients above the poverty line. Hence, elderly poverty rates fall to 0.3 percent or less. In the Social Security Out Plan, the elderly poverty rate would increase slightly to 7.0 percent in comparison to a rate of 6.8 percent under the current system.

TABLE 3
The Effect of the Current Tax Transfer System an

	Poverty Rate of Persons
Pretransfer,[1] Pretax[2]	22.43%
Posttransfer, Pretax	14.37%
Posttransfer, Posttax	14.41%
Current System[3] (100% value of benefits)	8.59%
Current System[4] (75% value of benefits)	10.01%
Current System[5] (50% value of benefits)	11.68%
Tax Rebate Plans	
Standard Plan[6]	
Before Labor Supply Change[7]	7.83%
After Labor Supply Change	2.56%
Child Plus Plan[8]	
Before Labor Supply Change	6.05%
After Labor Supply Change	1.57%
Single Parent Plus Plan[9]	
Before Labor Supply Change	6.81%
After Labor Supply Change	1.75%
Adult Plus Plan[10]	
Before Labor Supply Change	5.81%
After Labor Supply Change	1.81%
Social Security Out Plan[11]	
Before Labor Supply Change	6.97%
After Labor Supply Change	2.65%

Note:

1. Pretransfer: Before any Cash Transfer (including General Assistance) Programs.
2. Pretax: Before Federal Income Tax, Payroll Tax, and Earned Income Tax Credit.
3. Current System: Posttransfer, Posttax, and in-kind and all other programs except tax expenditures. The assumption is that the actual value of benefits from in-kind and other programs is 100 percent of face value of the benefit.
4. Same as 3, but the assumption is 75 percent of the face value.
5. Same as 3, but the assumption is 50 percent of the face value.
6. Standard Plan: Elderly $8,000, Adult $4,000, and Child $2,175 per year. OASDI kept harmless.

Poverty Rate of Children	Poverty Rate of the Elderly	Poverty Gap (Billions $)
25.72%	50.38%	189.68
21.70%	11.59%	79.75
21.21%	11.66%	78.06
12.06%	5.88%	34.05
14.55%	6.82%	42.15
17.29%	8.17%	52.27
13.47%	.29%	28.97
5.03%	.21%	10.78
8.09%	0%	23.66
2.05%	0%	9.45
10.26%	.13%	25.25
2.26%	.12%	10.39
11.28%	.30%	17.42
3.42%	.26%	7.97
11.28%	7.03%	20.71
3.75%	6.26%	9.71

i.e., people receive the tax rebate or OASDI, whichever is higher.

. Labor Change: Each poor able-bodied adult with the implementation of a tax rebate plan is assumed to have a part-time job (20 hours per week) at minimum wage ($5.15 per hour).

. Child Plus Plan: Elderly $8,000, Adult $3,150, and Child $4,000 per year. OASDI kept harmless.

. Single Parent Plus Plan: Elderly $8,000, First Adult with Children $6,000, Other Adult $3,000, and Child $2,700 per year. OASDI kept harmless.

0. Adult Plus: Elderly $8,000, Adult $6,000, and Child $2,000 per year. OASDI kept harmless.

1. Social Security Out Plan: Adult $6,000, and Child $2,000 per year. The recipients of OASDI and SSI are left out of tax rebate plan.

TABLE 4
The Effects of the Current Tax Transfer System and Tax Rebate Plans on the Vertical Income Distribution

	1st Quintile	2nd Quintile	3rd Quintile	4th Quintile	5th Quintile
Pretransfer,[1] Pretax[2]	.85%	7.16%	15.30%	26.32%	50.38%
Current System[3]	5.11%	10.60%	16.48%	25.14%	42.67%
Tax Rebate Plans					
Standard Plan[4]					
Before Labor Supply Change[5]	5.44%	10.86%	17.09%	25.26%	41.35%
After Labor Supply Change	6.07%	11.00%	16.99%	25.01%	40.94%
Child Plus Plan[6]					
Before Labor Supply Change	5.41%	10.84%	17.09%	25.33%	41.33%
After Labor Supply Change	5.94%	10.99%	17.00%	25.11%	40.96%
Single Parent Plus Plan[7]					
Before Labor Supply Change	5.39%	10.77%	17.17%	25.33%	41.34%
After Labor Supply Change	5.91%	11.02%	17.02%	25.11%	40.94%
Adult Plus Plan[8]					
Before Labor Supply Change	5.90%	11.18%	17.43%	25.31%	40.18%
After Labor Supply Change	6.35%	11.26%	17.36%	25.13%	39.90%
Social Security Out Plan[9]					
Before Labor Supply Change	5.85%	11.19%	17.44%	25.05%	39.49%
After Labor Supply Change	6.35%	11.31%	17.37%	24.87%	39.21%

Note:
1. Pretransfer: Before any Cash Transfer (including General Assistance) Programs.
2. Pretax: Before Federal Income Tax, Payroll Tax, and Earned Income Tax Credit.
3. Current System: Posttransfer, Posttax, and post-imputation of in-kind and all other programs except tax expenditures, using the assumption that actual value of in-kind and other program benefits is 75 percent of face value.
4. Standard Plan: Elderly $8,000, Adult $4,000, and Child $2,175 per year. OASDI kept harmless, i.e., people will get the tax rebate or OASDI, whichever is higher.
5. Labor Change: Each poor able-bodied adult with the implementation of tax rebate plans is assumed to have a part-time job (20 hours per week) at minimum wage ($5.15 per hour).
6. Child Plus Plan: Elderly $8,000, Adult $3,150, and Child $4,000 per year. OASDI kept harmless.
7. Single Parent Plus Plan: Elderly $8,000, First Adult with Children $6,000, Other Adult $3,000, and Child $2,700 per year. OASDI kept harmless.
8. Adult Plus Plan: Elderly $8,000, Adult $6,000, and Child $2,000 per year. OASDI kept harmless.
9. Social Security Out Plan: Adult $6,000, and Child $2,000 per year. The recipients of OASDI and SSI are left out of tax rebate plan.

The Effects on the Horizontal Distribution of Income

To simplify the discussion, Table 5 presents the results only for the simulations that include no labor supply increase. Except for the bottom quintile, the results are virtually identical for the labor supply increase simulations. The bottom quintile results, without the labor supply increase, are more conservative estimates of the gains to the poor.

Perhaps the most striking aspect of Table 5 is the large percentage of families in the first four income quintiles who experienced either significant increases or decreases in their incomes. In the Standard Plan, for example, over 80 percent of families in the bottom quintile gained or lost 10 percent or more, and the figures for the next three quintiles were 71 percent, 61 percent, and 46 percent. Note that within the first three quintiles, while more families gained than lost, a large minority of families in these quintiles experienced significant losses. In the Social Security Out Plan, there were far fewer losers in the first three quintiles than in the other plans. The results suggested that some of the OASDI and SSI beneficiaries receive significant income transfers along with substantial in-kind and imputed benefits from the current system.

TABLE 5
The Effects of the Current Tax Transfer System and Tax Rebate Plans on the Horizontal Income Distribution

	1st Quintile	2nd Quintile	3rd Quintile	4th Quintile	5th Quintile
Current System					
Percentage of Winners[1]	74.95%	53.17%	29.13%	14.50%	4.77%
Percentage of Losers[1]	7.25%	30.73%	55.00%	75.41%	84.82%
Mean Increase of Winners	$5,883	$9,512	$11,503	$12,441	$19,723
Mean Decrease of Losers	$1,597	$3,009	$5,093	$8,945	$22,695
Tax Rebate Plans[2]					
Standard Plan					
Percentage of Winners	47.06%	47.43%	43.58%	37.02%	5.78%
Percentage of Losers	36.01%	24.72%	17.02%	9.27%	6.06%
Winners' Mean Increase	$ 2,557	$3,269	$5,395	$6,227	$7,683
Losers' Mean Decrease	$3,164	$4,627	$7,245	$10,875	$15,745
Child Plus Plan					
Percentage of Winners	47.16%	31.06%	40.78%	37.52%	10.05%
Percentage of Losers	33.99%	25.50%	17.57%	9.68%	6.28%
Winners' Mean Increase	$2,241	$4,233	$5,816	$7,638	$7,880
Losers' Mean Decrease	$3,033	$4,547	$7,350	$10,797	$15,676
Single Parent Plus Plan					
Percentage of Winners	47.57%	30.50%	40.05%	39.95%	7.89%
Percentage of Losers	33.76%	25.55%	17.71%	9.91%	6.33%
Winners' Mean Increase	$2,116	$4,352	$6,059	$7,291	$7,266
Losers' Mean Decrease	$2,978	$4,559	$7,340	$10,674	$15,660
Adult Plus Plan					
Percentage of Winners	46.47%	60.14%	46.88%	44.45%	8.81%
Percentage of Losers	38.72%	23.90%	15.18%	8.99%	8.03%
Winners' Mean Increase	$3,551	$3,791	$6,603	$7,114	$8,624
Losers' Mean Decrease	$3,217	$5,737	$9,202	$12,605	$16,864
Social Security Out Plan					
Percentage of Winners	37.57%	44.63%	40.32%	33.85%	5.05%
Percentage of Losers	6.47%	2.45%	2.27%	6.74%	10.83%
Winners' Mean Increase	$3,708	$3,733	$6,505	$6,870	$8,883
Losers' Mean Decrease	$3,922	$4,856	$6,602	$6,250	$10,712

DATA AND METHODOLOGY

Microsimulation models provide useful tools for analyzing the effects of proposed changes in government programs, especially when the changes involve interactions between government programs and behavioral responses such as decisions to work. Therefore, we initially used a microsimulation model to estimate the effectiveness of existing anti-poverty measures. We then calculated the effectiveness of five proposed tax rebate plans in reducing poverty, decreasing the poverty gap, and redistributing income. The approach takes data on a large number of families and presents the way that current and then alternative government programs would apply to each individual described in the records (Citro and Hanushek, 1991).

Using specific employment, income, and demographic data on each of the 63,756 families in the Current Population Survey (CPS) sample, the microsimulation replaces the current level of cash, in-kind and other programs, and tax benefits (including personal exemptions) for each family in the sample with a tax rebate. To illustrate this, if a family of three receives AFDC, Food Stamps, and a housing subsidy, the income from these benefits would be subtracted from their current total income and replaced, in the Standard Plan, with $4,000 for the adult and $2,175 for each child, for a total rebate of $8,350 to this family. Each family in the sample is

Note:
1. Winners or losers are those with 10 percent more or less income than with the previous income base. The income base of current system is pretransfer and pretax, while the base of tax rebate plan is the current system.
2. All the numbers among alternative tax rebate plans are before labor supply changes.

treated individually, and the data are maintained as part of the total. This is a far more exacting way of examining the effects of policy on poverty than techniques based on aggregate information.

We used a seven-step procedure in each simulation, except for the Adult Plus Plan in which an eighth step was added. The steps of the microsimulation model are:

I. Select the Representative Population Database (1995 Current Population Survey).

II. Reconcile the Microdata from the CPS with Administrative Record Data.

III. Impute the Value of the In-Kind and Other Programs.

IV. Calculate the Value of the Current System (Post-transfer and Post-tax Income Plus In-Kind and Imputed Benefits) from Pretransfer and Pretax Income.

V. Eliminate the Current System.

VI. Simulate the Tax Rebate Plans.

VII. Adjust for Labor Supply Change of Poor People.

VIII. For Adult Plus Plan: Add in the Financing of the System.

STEP 1: *Select Representative Population Database—Current Population Survey*

This simulation is based on the March 1995 Current Population Survey database. The CPS, conducted by the U.S. Bureau of the Census, is a monthly cross-sectional survey of a large sample of the U.S. population. In the 1995 survey, CPS interviewed 63,756 families, which included 149,642 people. This sample is drawn from the U.S. population of 69 million families or 262 million people.

The survey contains data on labor force status and income for people, ages fifteen and older. Data collected for the basic CPS include demographic characteristics such as age, gender, race, marital status, and educational attainment, as well as labor force participation data such as usual weekly earnings, number of hours worked, and type of work. Annually, in March, supplemental employment and income-related data are collected, including use of public and private transfer programs and receipt of non-cash benefits, such as food stamps. Income-related data are based on income from the prior year.

The March 1995 Current Population Survey was selected because, of all the available databases, it could provide us with up-to-date,[*] comprehensive income-related information on a large sample of families—63,756 families.

STEP 2: *Reconcile the Microdata (CPS) with Administrative Record Data*

For the AFDC and Food Stamps programs, for example, discrepancies were noted in both the number of recipients and the aggregate costs between the data from the CPS and the administrative data recorded in *The 1993 Green Book* and *The 1995 Catalog of Federal Domestic Assistance*. We reconciled the data using the eligibility criteria described in *The 1993 Green Book*. Discrepancies are due, we believe, to underreporting of the receipt of benefits. Underreporting occurs when recipients do not report the benefit at all or report an amount lower than the actual amount of the benefit received. It may result from the stigma attached to receiving income-tested benefits.

If the number of recipients reported in CPS data was less than the number reported in *The 1993 Green Book,* we examined the CPS data to determine how many people who were eligible to receive the benefit did not report receiving it. If the number of recipients reporting the benefit, plus the number of eligible people-not-reporting, was equal to, or slightly higher than, the number reported in administrative data, we assumed conformity. CPS data count the number of recipients during the previous year. *Green Book* data are based on the average monthly recipients. We expected, therefore, that the imputed CPS data would be somewhat higher than the *Green Book* data.

STEP 3: *Impute the Value of the In-Kind and Other Programs to the CPS Data*

The value of most in-kind programs and of some other programs is not included in the CPS data. We, therefore, estimated the value of the benefits from these programs. This value was then added to each family's post-transfer and post-tax income to get the income of post-transfer, post-tax, and in-kind and imputed benefits. There are two parts to the calculation of in-kind and other programs:

(1) Determine the amount of in-kind and other program benefits that each family is likely to receive based on the budgeted amount. The allocation is based on the Incidence Assumption of each program. Six different allo-

cation methods were assumed because of the different methods that the programs use to distribute funds.

(2) Discount the amount calculated in the first step by a percentage to reflect the actual value of the benefit received. This reflects a discount for administrative costs and the fact that the actual value of in-kind benefits and services is lower than the value of cash. The Food Stamp program in 1993 was $26 billion, of which $3.2 billion was for administration costs. In addition, in-kind benefits or services are worth less to recipients than cash because their use is restricted. Therefore, the aggregated value of Food Stamps for these recipients is less than $22.8 billion. To determine what percentage would show up in the family income of recipients, we estimated the value of the in-kind and other programs at three levels: 100 percent, 75 percent, and 50 percent (see Table 5). The 100 percent and 50 percent assumptions allowed us to bracket the high and low projections, respectively. We used the 75 percent assumption, the intermediate projection, for the microsimulation, believing that this most accurately reflected the actual benefit.

STEP 4: *Calculate the Value of the Current System (Posttransfer and Post-tax Income Plus In-Kind and Imputed Benefits) from Pretransfer and Pretax Income*

The family income presented in the CPS data reflects all cash transfers, without incorporating tax liability. This is the post-transfer, pretax income. In this step, we first calculate the pretransfer, pretax income by subtracting all the cash-transfer benefits. Then, each family's tax liability for federal income tax, Earned Income Tax Credit (EITC), and payroll tax is deducted from the post-transfer, pretax income. We then distribute the in-kind benefits and other program benefits into post-tax, post-transfer income. This gives us the Current System, each family's post-transfer, post-tax income, plus in-kind and imputed benefits at the 100 percent, 75 percent, and 50 percent levels.

STEP 5: *Eliminate the Current System*
In this step we removed all the benefits of the current system from family income. We started by removing in-kind benefits and benefits from other programs from the current system income at the 75 percent assumption. Then, we deducted the tax exemptions and exclusions. Since the cash transfer benefits were included in the CPS data, we deducted the value of the benefit at the micro level directly, using CPS data.

STEP 6: *Simulate the Tax Rebate Plans*
In this step, we allotted the tax rebate benefits to each person. The criteria to determine the amount of tax rebate was based on age and family status, that is, whether you are an adult in a one- or a two-parent family. Recipients of OASDI are treated differentially depending on whether the rebate exceeds their OASDI benefits. In the Social Security Out Plan, the beneficiaries of OASDI and Supplemental Security Income (SSI) do not participate in the tax rebate plan and are exempt from cuts in benefits they receive from the federal government.

STEP 7: *Adjust for the Labor Supply Change of Poor People*
Step 6 produces family incomes before the labor supply

change. In step 7, we assume that 100 percent of the poor adults able to work will find part-time jobs (20 hours a week) at the minimum wage ($5.15 per hour) because the tax rebate plans do not penalize individuals who earn additional income. This new earned income is added to the family income to arrive at the "After Labor Supply Change" family income. In actuality, the true labor supply change will probably lie somewhere in between the 0 percent change and the change to part-time work. Our calculation merely provides lower and upper estimates.

STEP 8: *Add-in the Financing of the System (for the Adult Plus Plan and the Social Security Out Plan)*

In the Adult Plus Plan, the cost of the Tax Rebate Plan exceeded the cost of the current system by $233 billion. This could be financed by the states from state cuts in other benefits.

SUMMARY AND CONCLUSION

Tax rebates decrease poverty more effectively than the current system.

There are two cautions. First, though many of our imputation assumptions were relatively straightforward estimations (e.g., Headstart), we used approximate valuation methods in others. For example, in allocating Energy Assistance benefits, we assumed that only the poor recipients underreported; and for JPTA assumptions, we did not allocate benefits to elderly people or youth under eighteen, groups in which there are, in fact, recipients.

Additionally, the labor supply change assumption most likely overestimates the number of people who will go to work as a result of the tax rebate plan, and the values attributed to in-kind benefits may vary from the actual value of these benefits. We believe, however, that correcting these shortcomings will not change our fundamental results. Second, some of the programs replaced by the rebate may be worth keeping, because for each dollar spent they produce more than one dollar's worth of benefits.

The differences among the tax rebate plans are interesting, and we hope they will fuel debate about which variant is best. But the differences should not obscure the basic lesson. Tax rebates can reduce both government and poverty and provide meaningful middle-class tax relief.

*The Survey of Income and Program Participation (SIPP) has better income data but a smaller sample and is less up-to-date than the annual March CPS.

RESOURCES

Alaska Permanent Fund Corporation, "Alaskans Speak Out." (Alaska: Alaska Printing, 1995).

Anderson, Martin. *Welfare: The Political Economy of Welfare Reform in the United States*. (Palo Alto: Hoover Institution/Stanford University, 1978).

Feldstein, Martin. *Taxes and Capital Formation (National Bureau of Economic Research Project Report)*. (Chicago: University of Chicago, 1987).

Friedman, Milton. *Capitalism and Freedom*. (Chicago: University of Chicago Press, 1963).

Friedman, Milton. *Free to Choose: A Personal Statement*. (New York: Harcourt Brace, 1990).

Friedman, Milton. *Tax Limitation, Inflation and the Role of Government*. (Dallas: Fisher Institute, 1979).

Garfinkel, Irwin. "Effects of a Tax Rebate on Poverty and Income Distribution." (Institute for SocioEconomic Studies Perspective, July 1997).

Gilder, George. *Wealth & Poverty*. (San Francisco: Institute for Contemporary Studies, 1993).

Greene, Leonard M. *Free Enterprise Without Poverty*. (New York: W.W. Norton, 1981).

Hall, Robert E. *Fairness and Efficiency in the Flat Tax*. (Washington, DC: AEI Press, 1996).

Hall, Robert E. and Alvin Rabushka. *Flat Tax*. (Stanford: Hoover Institute Press, 1995).

Hayek, F. A. *The Road to Serfdom*. (Chicago: University of Chicago Press, 1944).

Kaplan, H. Roy. *Lottery Winners: How They Won and How Winning Changed Their Lives*. (New York: Harper and Row, 1981).

Murray, Charles. *In Pursuit of Happiness and Good Government*. (New York: Simon and Schuster, 1988).

Murray, Charles. *Losing Ground: American Social Policy 1950-1980*. (New York: Basic Books, 1984).

Olasky, Marvin. *The Tragedy of American Compassion*. (New York: Basic Books, 1992).

O'Rourke, P. J. "Parliament of Whores." (New York: *The Atlantic Monthly*, 1991).

Reagan, Ronald. *An American Life*. (New York: Simon and Schuster, 1990).

Tanner, Michael. *The End of Welfare: Fighting Poverty in the Civil Society*. (Washington, DC: Cato Institute, 1996).

Tanner, Michael, Stephen Moore, and David Hartman. "The Work vs. Welfare Trade-Off: An Analysis of the Total Level of Welfare Benefits by State." (Cato Institute Policy Analysis no. 240, September 19, 1996).

---

[1] The Survey of Income and Program Participation (SIPP) has better income data but a smaller sample and is less up-to-date than the annual March CPS.

THE INSTITUTE FOR SocioEconomic Studies (ISES) is a nonprofit think tank based in White Plains, New York. The mission of the Institute is to educate and promote understanding in areas such as the quality of life, social motivation, poverty, urban regeneration, and the problems of the elderly, primarily as they relate to domestic government policy. Since its founding in 1974 by Leonard M. Greene, the Institute has been exploring approaches to comprehensive welfare reform, work incentives, health care reform, and related social policy issues. Through its publications, seminars, and special initiatives, the institute has been successful in providing a national forum for the dissemination of information and the free exchange of ideas.

LEONARD M. GREENE is a remarkable innovator whose creative thinking and inventions have made an indelible contribution to the advancement of society and aviation. For thirty years, he has been deeply concerned with America's social problems, convinced that eradication of poverty is not only possible, but also essential to preserving our free enterprise system. As founder of the Institute for SocioEconomic Studies (ISES), he has conducted original research and advanced breakthrough ideas on poverty reform, senior issues, urban regeneration, and health care reform. Greene's foresight led to ISES becoming among the first U.S. policy organizations to host Margaret Thatcher.

Greene has pursued a lifelong interest in aviation. During the Second World War, he presented the first formula for breaking the sound barrier, years before the first experiments that made supersonic flight possible. After the war, he started the Safe Flight Instrument Corporation to manufacture and market his invention, the Stall Warning Indicator. Called "the greatest lifesaver since the invention of the parachute" by the *Saturday Evening Post*, the

Stall Warning Indicator received the Flight Safety Foundation's first Air Safety Award. Stall Warning Indicators are found on all aircrafts today. Responding to another potentially deadly threat to aviation safety, Greene invented and patented the first Wind Shear Warning System in 1976. For these and numerous other break-throughs—he has received more than one hundred patents—Greene was awarded the 1976 Flight Safety Foundation Award for Meritorious Service and the 1996 National Business Aircraft Association Award for Meritorious Service. He was inducted into the National Inventors Hall of Fame in 1991.

Greene co-founded the Corporate Angel Network, which makes corporate planes available to transport cancer patients free of charge to and from distant hospitals. He also established the Chain Scholarship Foundation, a scholarship program for college seniors who pledged to repay their scholarships for the benefits of future college seniors. He has testified before Congress and has been a Council Member in the U.S. Chamber of Commerce.

Greene is author of the book, *Free Enterprise Without Poverty* (W.W. Norton, 1981), and has been widely published in numerous magazines and newspapers across the country. He holds degrees in engineering from City College–City University of New York and was awarded an honorary Doctor of Civil Law by Pace University.

dependents, 71

E

economy, 19, 26, 96

education, 91-93

Earned Income Tax Credit, 48, 56-57, 72

entrepreneurs, 32, 43, 96-98

entry level job, 32

expenses, 52-53, 61-64, 72-83, 86-90

experience, 28, 32

F

family: effect of welfare on, 12; role of man in, 11, 89

farmers, 98

Ferrara, Peter, 17

flat tax, 19, 21, 22

Forest Service, U.S., 7

Freedom and Fairness Restoration Act of 1997, 21

Fortune 500 Companies, 26

founding fathers, 30-31

freedom, 27, 48

free enterprise, 29

Friedman, Milton, 12

G

Garfinkel, Irwin, 85

General Accounting Office, 55-56

Gilder, George, 33

government: accountability, 34; business and, 10, 27; control, 6, 9, 10, 83, 95; evil of, xi; freedom and, 11, 22, 83, 97; growth of, 6, 10, 22, 25, 46, 95; inefficiency of, 68, 96; middleman, 68; money management in, 63-64; proper use of, 36; reduction of, 22, 27, 85, 90, 99, 103; waste of, 68, 96, 97

government programs, in-kind, 14, 38, 42, 73-74, 105, 106, 113, 116-17

government spending, 3, 6; abuse of, 3, 7, 9, 22, 34, 46, 66

Gramm, Phil, 31

Great Depression, 5, 8

Green Book, 37

guaranteed income, 41

H

Hall, Ralph, 20

Hammond, Governor Jay, 58

history, 47

hope, 70, 82

horizontal distribution of income, 111-12

human nature, 29

I

illegitimacy, 11, 15

income tax, 21

income, investment, 21, 54

income, needs for: 52-53, 61-64, 72-83, 86-90

inventors, 26

industries, 26

individual: freedom of, 31, 33-34, 48, 83, 90; trust in, 84; importance of, 27, 28, 30-31

incentives: 4, 23; human nature and, 29, 40-41, 48; work

THE NATIONAL TAX REBATE